# THE BIBLE

# WHAT DOES IT REALLY SAY ?

# THE BIBLE

WHAT DOES IT REALLY SAY?

Exploring the reality
behind the assumptions

## H. J. Richards

First published in 1999 by
KEVIN MAYHEW LTD
Buxhall
Stowmarket
Suffolk IP14 3BW

0 1 2 3 4 5 6 7 8 9

ISBN 1 84003 457 2
Catalogue Number 1500319

Cover illustration by Jonathan Stroulger
Edited by Helen Elliot
Typesetting by Kevin Whomes
Printed and bound in Great Britain

# Contents

# Preface

The word 'really' in my title is meant to link this book with other titles of mine. In all of them I have been searching for the reality lying behind our formulas and creeds, our beliefs and unexamined assumptions. What *really* happened at the first Christmas and the first Easter, as distinct from what people imagine or presume? What *really* lies behind the miracle stories of Jesus? What will *really* happen when we die? What *really* happens when we ask for things in prayer?

Not that I can offer a pat answer to these questions. The question mark in my chapter headings is deliberate and should not be mistaken for a full stop. I don't mind asking many more questions than I can answer. Nonetheless, I am convinced that the search for the real as distinct from the imaginary remains worthwhile. It can pinpoint more accurately what it is that Christians really commit themselves to.

In this book I am asking questions about the real meaning of the Bible. Not of the whole Bible, obviously! Who would be able to do that? Indeed, who would want to do that, given that the Bible itself continues to speak more clearly and powerfully, thank God, than any commentary?

But the Bible does not always speak with one voice on every topic. It would be quite remarkable if it did, given that it is the work of so many authors spread across so many centuries. The book of Jonah does not speak with the voice of Nahum, nor the Gospel of John with that of Mark. Nor were those who collected all these writings into a single volume disturbed by these differences; they were presumably content to let them bear witness to the 'many and various ways' in which God spoke to our forbears. It seems to me that those who claim to respect the Bible should acknowledge this pluriformity, and not pretend that there is a single Bible teaching on all the topics it deals with.

But out of respect for the Bible they should go even further and acknowledge the relative nature of the Bible, and not turn it into an absolute. Even if the Bible spoke with one consistent voice on all its topics, its words would still be limited by the thought-patterns of those who wrote it. They were people living from the tenth century BC to the first century AD, not timeless people from outer space. And the fact that they wrote in one particular age, not in an ageless age, limits them just as surely as the words we speak and write today are limited by the thought patterns of our century. How could it be otherwise? If God wishes to communicate with human beings by embodying his Word in human form, then he cannot do other than accept the human limitations involved. The alternative is no human Word of God. Only God remains absolute. If his Word is to be heard, it must be heard through (and not identified with) the human writings in which he speaks to us.

It is these twin concerns for the pluriform and the relative which form a link between the chapters that follow, even though they cover a wide variety of topics. They represent some of the biblical material on which I have been asked to write articles, give lectures or lead discussion groups across the years. Many of the pieces have grown in the process and some have been re-cast several times. All of them have been revised for this publication, which is why I do not give them an attribution or a date.

Some of the chapters repeat points made in previous chapters, while others may seem to be in considerable tension with each other. I do not apologise for this. The Bible has many points of view, and I do not claim to have the wisdom to reconcile them, only the determination to try to hold them in tension. My hope in putting them together in this collection is that they may still have something to say to those who ask, as I do, what does the Bible really say?

Biblical quotations, except where indicated, are taken from the Revised Standard Version.

# Introduction

## *What does the Bible really say?*

At a Roman Catholic funeral service I attended, the first reading was a lovely piece from the (apocryphal) book of Wisdom:

> The souls of the righteous are in the hand of God,
> and no torment will ever touch them.
> In the eyes of the foolish they seemed to have died,
> and their departure was thought to be an affliction,
> and their going from us to be their destruction;
> but they are at peace.
> For though in the sight of men they were punished,
> their hope is full of immortality.
> Having been disciplined a little, they will receive great good,
> because God tested them and found them worthy of himself;
> like gold in the furnace he tried them,
> and like a sacrificial burnt offering he accepted them.
> In the time of their visitation they will shine forth ...
> and the Lord will reign over them for ever ...
> because grace and mercy are upon his elect,
> and he watches over his holy ones.
> (Wisdom 3:1-9)

## *Divine guarantee?*

The reading ended, as is the custom, with the proclamation: 'This is the Word of the Lord', and we dutifully responded: 'Thanks be to God', or in other words, 'We're most grateful'.

Now, although I really was grateful, and wanted these words to have the divine *imprimatur* because they are most consoling, I actually found myself wondering whether this literally was the Word of the Lord. What I mean is this. Not only do some other books of the Bible refuse to give such a consoling message (some are quite categorical that nothing awaits us beyond the grave), but disagreements on important matters are to be found within the pages of a single author. Paul, for example, was quite certain in his early letters that the Second Coming of Christ would take place within his own lifetime; in later letters he changed his mind.

So which of the two, this author or that, an author's earlier statement or his later one, is the Word of God? Which of the two has the divine guarantee, carrying absolute and final authority?

Nor is that the only problem. Supposing that none of the biblical authors ever changed his mind, but always said exactly the same thing throughout his writings; and supposing that none of the authors were in tension with any other, but were all totally consistent. Even so, how entitled would I be to take these single-minded and consistent statements of theirs as the absolute Word of God? Do I not have to make allowance for the background against which these statements were first made? Do I not have to take into consideration the culture in which they were written, the world-view of the time, the thought-patterns of the authors, their limitations, their likes and dislikes, their inevitable ignorance of certain things, their education, their philosophy, their priorities, their prejudices? Surely all these have deeply influenced their thinking, if not actually dictated it?

## Ways of thinking

To return to the book of Wisdom. It was in fact written by a pious Jew living in Egypt in the first century BC, a time when Jews living abroad were being deeply influenced by Greek philosophy. This philosophy, unlike all Hebrew thinking before or since, worked on the assumption that people could be split up into two parts, their bodies which eventually died, and their 'souls' which lived on ('the *souls* of the righteous', 'they *seemed* to have died', 'full of *immortality*'). The distinction was a useful one for solving the age-old problem of evil. If anyone asked why a just God does not reward virtue and punish evil, you could reply, 'He will, don't you worry, once the soul has been separated from the body.' And it is this way of thinking that the author of the book of Wisdom has adopted.

But this way of thinking is *only* a way of thinking. It has been pretty influential in the West ever since it was first proposed in fourth century BC Greece. But it has always been questioned by some people, and has been radically questioned for the last two hundred years. As a person living some thousands of years later, how am I supposed to react to this way of thinking as I find it embodied in Scripture?

What I am asking is this. If I accept a piece of Scripture as the Word of God, do I have to accept its packaging as well? Am I obliged to share its author's world-view, even if this does violence to my own? Or am I allowed to distinguish between what the author is most profoundly trying to say, and the particular philosophy in which he expresses himself?

I say, 'Am I allowed?' Surely I am bound to make that distinction. Surely this is no mere permission granted to me, but an obligation. Surely calling something the 'Word of God' cannot mean repeating it mechanically for ever and ever. Surely something that is to be the Word of God *for me* will involve asking the most searching questions. Surely I will have to ask: 'If that author, living at that time, immersed in that culture, thinking with that mentality, saw God's relationship to people in those terms – then how must I see my relationship to God, living as I do in my time, immersed in my culture, and thinking with my utterly different mentality?'

Putting it more simply, the proclamation, 'This is the Word of the Lord' does not mean: 'This, word for word, literally, as it stands, is what God is saying to me here and now, and if I bite it anywhere I will find the word 'GOD' written all the way through.' It means something more like, 'God speaks to me through this reading, and by means of it'. And perhaps the proclamation at the end of the reading should not be, 'This is the Word of the Lord', but 'Listen for the Word of the Lord'. Because what God may actually be saying to me could be something very different from what is being said at the lectern – as I have frequently discovered in being at the receiving end of sermons.

## Critical thinking

For a Christian of this century, the Bible has become a very complex reality. The last two hundred years have seen a veritable revolution in biblical studies. True enough, the revolution was resisted at every turn. But it has changed things, and only ostriches are now able to pretend that it has not taken place. I am referring to the literary and historical criticism of the Bible, which began to be taken seriously towards the end of the eighteenth century, and has been gathering steam and gaining strength ever since, especially over the last hundred years.

*Literary criticism* is concerned with reconstructing, as accurately as possible, all the circumstances in which a piece of writing was first composed: the background, the culture, the ideas, the sources, the influences, the copying and borrowing, the subsequent editing, and so on. *Historical criticism* is part of this work. It is concerned with placing a piece of writing accurately within its historical context. It works on the assumption that no literature comes to us out of the blue. Whatever else we may wish to say about it, it is not timeless, but the product of its age.

When it was first suggested that the Bible ought to be subjected to this kind of criticism, some people were profoundly shocked. The Bible, surely, is one piece of literature which *does* come to us out of the blue! The Bible, surely, is unique in literature, and cannot be measured and assessed as if it were simply another Homer, or Virgil, or Shakespeare!

But in spite of all the protests raised by good Christians, the naughty scholars went ahead with their critical approach. And they did it with such thoroughness and assurance that eventually the good Christians themselves became the most radical in their criticism.

The results are common knowledge. We resisted the conclusions for a long time, but we have gradually become used to them. We now know, for example, that the creation of the world did not take six days, as the book of Genesis seemed to imply; the account it gives is not a piece of divinely revealed science at all, and must be presumed to be something else. We now know that the Pentateuch was not written by Moses, who lived in 1300 BC, but is an intricate patchwork or mosaic of four clearly defined sources, of which the latest was written a thousand years after Moses. We now know that the Assyrian Empire was not miraculously converted by Jonah and his whale; the book turns out to be not a history but a satire. We now know that the prophet Isaiah did not marvellously write about events which in his time (700 BC) were still two hundred years in the future; this part of the book of Isaiah was added by another hand, around 500 BC. We now know that the book of Daniel is not a cryptic foretelling of events stretching from the Babylonian Exile (600 BC) down to Maccabee times; it was actually written by a Maccabee in the 200s and was made deliberately cryptic so that it would look like a foretelling.

In short, we now know that the Bible can no longer be read, as it used to be, in one tone of voice throughout. It is not one book but a whole library of books, where history jostles with fiction, and law books with love poems, and sermons with private diaries, and formal theological articles

13

with letters written off the cuff. Each has to be read in a different tone of voice. Each (to vary the metaphor) has to be played in a different musical key. To play them all in the same key, or to mistake the key in which the piece was meant to be played, is to create disharmony. Nor does it make matters easier that some biblical pieces were written in 'keys' which are no longer in use today.

## Gospel criticism

The critical approach of which I have been speaking applies, of course, not only to the Old Testament, but to the New Testament as well. There was a time when Christian scholars happily applied the most radical criticism to the Genesis stories, but never dreamt that the logic of the situation demanded that the Gospel stories must be subjected to the same treatment. 'These, surely, are a special case', they said. But why should they be?

All New Testament scholars are agreed that the Gospels are not the simple and straightforward documents we once took them to be. They are made up of many strands, of which the historical fact ('what really happened?') is only one. More important than the historical fact is the author's own interpretation of Jesus. None of the writers presents an objective or neutral picture of Jesus such as any uncommitted observer could have provided. Each one is obviously concerned to present 'Jesus as I see him', 'what Jesus means for me'. The result is that the Gospels do not give us one consistent picture of Jesus, but at least four. And there is no reason why these should agree with each other at every point.

This means, of course, that the reported words of Jesus are not necessarily what he actually said, but what Matthew, Mark, Luke and John interpreted them to mean forty, fifty, sixty or seventy years later. Certainly there are few New Testament scholars who any longer imagine that Jesus personally said, 'Before Abraham was I am', or, 'Learn from me, for I am meek and humble of heart', or, 'I am the Resurrection and the Life'.

This does not make such texts worthless. Since they express most powerfully what Jesus continues to mean for the believer, they are the most valuable of all the Gospel texts. But if they could not have been captured on a tape-recorder, we are not entitled to quote them as if they could have been. We may no longer read the Gospels as naïvely as we once did. They are no longer as absolute as they once were.

## *Relativising Jesus*

What worries some people more deeply still is that, in the light of this critical approach, even Jesus is no longer as absolute as he once was. Yet it stands to reason that, whatever we may ultimately wish to say about him, he was a man of his time, and therefore limited in his viewpoint like every other person living in time. Christians are very serious about professing that, in Jesus of Nazareth, God 'became man'. But few are serious about accepting the consequences of such a belief. If Jesus was truly a man, then he did not simply *look* like a Jew of the first century: that is what he *was*. He could do no other than live and react and think like other people of his time. So that even if we can accurately pinpoint some of the Gospel sayings as actually the words of Jesus, even these may not be absolutised. They too cannot be other than culturally conditioned.

To take some actual examples. People of the first century thought of the earth as being flat, and fixed at the centre of the universe, with the sun and moon circling around it. Jesus would have thought like that. Are there still people who imagine that they have to share that viewpoint? People of the first century thought that certain sicknesses like epilepsy were due to possession by an evil spirit, and could only be cured by exorcism. Jesus would have thought like that. Are there still people who imagine that they have to share that viewpoint? Jews of the first century thought of Kingdom Come as something imminent, and expected it to be brought about by a visible intervention of God. It is possible, perhaps probable, that Jesus thought like that. Are there still people who imagine that they have to share that viewpoint, so late in the day?

## Losses and gains

There are two consequences to be drawn from this critical approach to the Bible, one negative and one positive.

*Negatively*, it means that we can no longer be as naïve about the Bible as we once were. I can no longer regard the Bible as 'the Word of God full stop', which tells me exactly what to believe and what to do. The crib in Bethlehem was not the best of all possible cribs. The conditions in Nazareth were not the best of all possible conditions. And the words of the Bible are not the best of all possible words.

This means that even if I can work out accurately and precisely what was meant by the psalmist, or by Isaiah, or by Paul, this does not automatically bind me as I once thought it did. The psalmist is entitled to his opinion, as are Isaiah and Paul. I can no longer quote the Bible with the rubric, 'Scripture teaches', or 'The Bible commands', or 'We are told', or 'The Gospel forbids us', or 'Paul orders us'. He doesn't. The Word of God no longer comes to us direct from the text. The text is no longer an absolute. It has been relativised. We shall have to find new words to express our belief in the inspiration, and inerrancy, and authority of the Bible. How astonished Paul would be to find that for nineteen hundred years we had absolutised the social convention of his day, that women should wear hats in church!

Some may regard this relativisation of the Bible as a loss. But it has its positive aspect.

*Positively,* it means that the Word of God comes to us in a thoroughly human form. God speaks to us, not by means of a divine broadcast from heaven, but in the voices and thoughts and ideas of our fellow human beings. Our God is not to be found in what is extraordinary or odd or unusual, but in what is ordinary, usual and normal. The Word of God, and the presence of God, have become truly incarnate.

This can, of course, be a disappointment for those who would prefer a clear voice addressed to them out of a clear blue sky. The kind of Word of God I have been describing is not clear. It is ambiguous, indirect, oblique and problematical. Worse, it makes great demands on me. It no longer solves my problems, or saves me the bother of thinking. I can no longer consult Moses, or David, or Hosea, or Matthew, or Paul, or even Jesus, to tell me what to do. Instead, I have to ask, 'If Moses, or David, or Hosea, or Matthew, or Paul, or even Jesus, thinking as they did, saw their relationship to God in those terms, in what terms must I see it, thinking as I do?' God's revelation is no longer contained in Scripture, as in a carrier bag. It is only reflected there, through the eyes of its writers.

Yet when that reflection hits me, when what God spoke in the lives of the biblical authors shines into my life and enlightens me, then indeed God speaks to me through the medium of the Bible. And if for some people it is worrying that God's Word should come to them in such a roundabout way, they ought eventually to be consoled. Because when they think about it, they will realise that this is how God has always spoken to people, and continues to do so. It is not only in the Bible that God's voice can be heard, but in all the events of people's lives. It is not only Jews and Christians who hear the Word of God.

Then why put such emphasis on the Bible, for heaven's sake? If God speaks in all the events of the lives of all people, why should I accord the Bible such a privileged place?

Because this is the story of the pilgrimage of faith made by the people I belong to. This is where my family have borne witness to their faith, and told what they saw and heard of God. And although I can't make their faith a substitute for mine – that has to be my own – I need the richness of their thinking to feed me, to challenge me, and to rebuke the thin, trivial, superficial, inadequate, self-centred, narrow and destructive ideas I call my own. It is through the witness of the biblical authors, reflected into me and reflected upon by me, that God continues to speak. Thank God for that, because without that witness I wouldn't know who I was.

How has this family of mine borne witness to its faith when it faced the kind of problems I have to face today – war and peace, poverty and providence, faith and forgiveness, and the rest? Can God still speak to me through their witness? The chapters which follow try to offer some guidelines.

### Questions for Discussion

- Does 'relativising' the Bible (see the examples given in this chapter) leave you feeling disturbed or relieved? Explain why.

- Do the more positive results of modern biblical criticism (as outlined in the final paragraphs above) make up for the sense of loss in no longer having 'a clear voice addressed to us out of a clear blue sky'?

- If the Bible can be misunderstood as easily as is suggested in this chapter, was not the medieval Church wise in restricting people's access to it?

# 1. On poverty:
## *how blessed are the poor?*

What does the Bible say about the unfortunate, the unsuccessful, the unfulfilled, the under-privileged? About the weak, the needy, the wretched, the miserable, the deprived, the destitute, the distressed? About the afflicted, the oppressed, the persecuted, the downtrodden, the lowly?

### *Many insights*

The Bible has quite a bit to say on this subject, which is not surprising, since it was written by the poor for the poor. Ancient literature is filled with stories of kings and princes, of chieftains and nobles. The Bible alone tells the long history of the poor and persecuted, of the weeping and suffering, from the blood of Abel calling out from the ground, to the hungry crowds on whom Jesus had pity. The stereotype of the Jew as a miserly moneybags is the very opposite of the image offered by the Bible, where he is a member of an eternally poor and downtrodden people. Jewish humour echoes this self-image. 'God must love the poor,' says one wit, 'he made so many of us.' 'If the poor could die for the rich,' speculates another, 'they could make a very good living.'

Because it has so much to say on the subject of poverty, the Bible approaches it from many different angles. There is no reason why these angles should coincide with each other. A literature which is the work of so many hands across so many centuries is bound to contain many insights, and it would be reasonable to expect it to propose several views about poverty, not only one. To find a text and quote it with the rubric, 'This is what the Bible says about poverty,' is dishonest, if there are a dozen other texts which say something quite different. Honesty demands that we look at a fair sample of all of them, before making any judgement. Above all we should avoid oversimplification. It is an oversimplification, at one extreme, so to idealise poverty that any kind of prosperity, or health, or security becomes suspect, as if the only people God loves are the unsuccessful. It is an oversimplification, at the other extreme, so to fear poverty that it becomes essential to avoid it all costs, as if it had no redeeming features. The two views are opposites. They cannot both be right. They could both be wrong.

### Poverty as a curse

Strangely, it is with the negative view of poverty that the Bible begins its thinking on this matter. The first thing it has to say about deprivation and misfortune is that they are a curse.

How can anyone be neutral about something so obviously contrary to our wellbeing, less still welcome it? Suffering diminishes people, restricts them, prevents them becoming fully human. People must resist it, and do battle against it not only for themselves but on behalf of all their brothers and sisters. Health and wealth are not to be regarded as suspect. On the contrary, they are what living is all about, and those who are lucky enough to have them are obviously blessed by God.

So the biblical story starts with Abraham as a model of wealth and success. A later tradition loved to see him as an example of the poor homeless wanderer, but the book of Genesis presents him as a very prosperous and successful Bedouin, rich in wives and in property: 'he had sheep, oxen, he-asses, menservants, maidservants, she-asses and camels... and was very rich in cattle, in silver and in gold.' (Genesis 12:16 – 13:2) Such prosperity was a sign that God was on his side.

The Exodus story that follows is meant to illustrate the same theme. The people of Abraham have been reduced to poverty: that must be changed. They have been brought low with misfortune: that must be reversed. They have met with failure: that must be transformed into success. And when it is, it proves that God is on their side.

And it is the same with the rest of Israel's history. Whenever there is a reversal of good fortune, it is interpreted as a sign that God has withdrawn his favour. It is folly to imagine that God wants his people to be poor and deprived: on the contrary, poverty and deprivation are seen precisely as his punishment. If he shows himself to be on the side of the destitute, it is not because he wants to confirm them in that state, but the very opposite. He is on their side to rescue them from destitution. What he wants for them is a full life, a rich life, a free life. Poverty is evil.

There are plenty of Old Testament texts to illustrate this negative aspect of poverty. One of the most moving is in the book of Job:

> Why are not times of judgement kept by the Almighty?...
> Men remove landmarks; they seize flocks and pasture them.
> They drive away the ass of the fatherless;
>     they take the widow's ox for a pledge.
> They thrust the poor off the road;
>     the poor of the earth all hide themselves.
> Behold, like wild asses in the desert they go forth to their toil,
>     seeking ... food for their children.
> They gather their fodder in the field
>     and they glean the vineyard of the wicked man.
> They lie all night naked, without clothing,
>     and have no covering in the cold.
> They are wet with the rain of the mountains,
>     and cling to the rock for want of shelter...
> They go about naked, without clothing;
>     hungry, they carry the sheaves;
> among the olive rows of the wicked they make oil;
>     they tread the wine presses, but suffer thirst.

From out of the city the dying groan,
>   and the soul of the wounded cries for help;
>   yet God pays no attention to their prayer.
(Job 24:1-12 NJB)

Who could read such a passage and say, 'Isn't that beautiful?' Kingdom Come will be when that sort of situation is no longer possible. God could not be God if he approved of such a situation. He can only be God if he is the avenger of the needy, the deliverer of the poor, the saviour of the downtrodden and afflicted. As the following texts witness:

> You shall not wrong a stranger or oppress him, for you were strangers in the land of Egypt. You shall not afflict any widow or orphan. If you do afflict them, and they cry out to me, I will surely hear their cry… If ever you take your neighbour's garment in pledge, you shall restore it to him before the sun goes down; for that is his only covering, it is his mantle for his body; in what else shall he sleep? And if he cries to me, I will hear, for I am compassionate.
> (Exodus 22:21-23, 26-27)

> O Lord, who is like thee,
> thou who deliverest the weak
> from him who is too strong for him,
> the weak and needy from him
> who despoils him?
> (Psalm 35:10)

> The earth feared and was still,
> when God arose to establish judgement,
> to save all the oppressed of the earth.
> (Psalm 76:8-9)

> O Lord, thou God of vengeance,
> thou God of vengeance, shine forth!
> Rise up, O judge of the earth;
> render to the proud their deserts!

O Lord, how long shall the wicked,
how long shall the wicked exult?
They pour out their arrogant words,
they boast, all the evildoers.
They crush thy people, O Lord,
and afflict thy heritage.
They slay the widow and the sojourner,
and murder the fatherless;
and they say, 'The Lord does not see;
the God of Jacob does not perceive'.
(Psalm 94:1-7)

Sing to the Lord; praise the Lord!
For he has delivered the life of the needy
from the hand of evildoers.
(Jeremiah 20:13)

The suffering psalms, however loudly they inveigh against God, all presume that he will deliver the destitute and reverse their misfortune. The Messiah is awaited precisely as the defender of the poor and the healer of sickness. The Kingdom of God will have come when the poor are rescued from their poverty, the downtrodden freed, the sick cured, and the maladjusted adjusted, not left in their wretchedness. The book of Isaiah puts it in these words:

God's spirit is in my heart,
he has called me and set me apart;
this is what I have to do:
He's sent me to give the good news to the poor,
tell prisoners that they are prisoners no more,
tell blind people that they can see,
and set the downtrodden free,
and go tell everyone
the news that the Kingdom of God has come.
(Isaiah 61:1-2, tr. H. J. Richards)

## Jesus' manifesto

The New Testament takes up those very words as the manifesto under which Jesus of Nazareth begins his preaching career. He proclaims that the Kingdom of God has come precisely because the poor and afflicted are going to stop being afflicted.

People sometimes sentimentalise poverty, as if the New Testament proposed it as something virtuous. But Jesus was not himself a poor man. To be the village carpenter or builder was a very comfortable middle-class profession. The tax-gatherers he consorted with were the prosperous people of his day. Those who adopted a poor lifestyle were the Pharisees, and with many of these he found himself at loggerheads. The stories he told depicted the poor Pharisees as ungodly and much further away from God than the wealthy tax-gatherers. The poverty he came across in the sick and disabled was not something of which he approved: he did all in his power to get rid of it.

Even the *Magnificat,* on the opening page of Luke's Gospel, says something quite different from what people imagine it to say. When it is sung by tremulous boy trebles in a cathedral evensong, it can movingly suggest humility and resignation. But in the raw, it is a recipe for revolution:

He has shown strength with his arm,
he has scattered the proud in the imagination of their hearts,
he has put down the mighty from their thrones,
and exalted those of low degree;
he has filled the hungry with good things,
and the rich he has sent empty away.
(Luke 1:51-53)

That kind of talk does not call for the resigned acceptance of deprivation, but for rebellion.

It is in the light of this attitude that we must read the history of Judaism and Christianity, as a perpetual campaign to fight poverty. Poverty of any kind – physical, intellectual, spiritual – is not something that Jews and Christians have stood back to admire. They have waded in to eliminate it. And still do so, from CAFOD and OXFAM down to the parochial Society of St Vincent de Paul.

## More positive

And perhaps it is at this point that something more positive needs to be said. We have considered many texts which see only the negative aspects of poverty. Has the Bible anything more positive to offer?

Indeed. For if Scripture is so insistent that God is concerned for the poor and oppressed and underprivileged, that he does not stand idly by, but places himself alongside them, then I as a believer have to ask myself where I stand. If I stand idly by, if I show unconcern, if I do not identify with the poor in the way that God is always shown to do, then I may find myself at odds with God. I cannot simply stand alongside the rich and healthy, the successful and wealthy, and hope that God is with me. He is standing over there, alongside the others. That should give me pause for thought.

It is this consideration, of course, that lies behind the thinking of Liberation theologians, who have no hesitation in urging Christian leaders to be involved in the political struggle for people's freedom. When they are accused of exchanging the Gospel for a brand of Marxism, they can only point to the many texts which speak of God's preferential option for the poor. No one who wishes to remain on God's side can stand on the sidelines, less still remain an uncritical part of the system which oppresses the poor.

But there is an even deeper point to be made. The poor and deprived whom God stands alongside are not only his protégés; in some mysterious way they have become his friends. Poverty arouses not simply God's pity and compassion, but his friendship. The state of deprivation brings about a closeness to God, an intimacy and union with God, which no amount of health and wealth can do. The psalmist sums it up neatly:

> Before I was afflicted I went astray.
> (Psalm 119:67)

This means, 'I only went in the right direction after being afflicted and because of it. Suffering brought me to God, and allowed me to know God more deeply than I could ever have done without suffering.' Why should this be so? We need to analyse the matter more closely.

## The Prophets

In the 1950s, the Abbé Pierre received a lot of publicity for his work among the rag-pickers of Paris. He had gone to live among these poorest of the poor with the aim of lifting them out of the gutter, giving dignity to their lives, and restoring them to normal society. What shattered him, and eventually made him abandon the work, was the discovery that the poor wretches he had rescued were not in the least interested in putting themselves out to help others in the same plight. Once they had emerged from the gutter and made it back into normal society, they acted like everyone else in normal society, and asked to be left in peace. Merely reversing their roles had not changed their attitudes. Only an on-going positive understanding of poverty is able to achieve that.

In the 1981 Naples earthquake, which killed two thousand and made many more homeless, a local bishop spoke of how moved he was by the way all the survivors happily shared what little food and clothing they had; and how distressed he was by the way they reverted to a more selfish way of life as soon as relief workers brought in supplies. Until deeper attitudes are changed, nothing is changed.

This is what some of the Old Testament prophets began to understand as early as the seventh century BC. They had no illusions about the negative aspects of poverty and deprivation, and were as ready as anyone else to do battle against them. But they also began to see that poverty could have a positive aspect. It could bring people to a realisation that everyone stands as a beggar before God. It could even bring them to begin seeing the world through the eyes of the deprived.

By the seventh century BC, Israel's prosperous days were over. The majority of the population lived under conditions of considerable poverty. The prophets asked whether this was necessarily a total disaster. If you ate anything in a situation like that, you at least knew that you ate out of God's hands. Poverty and distress, dependence and insecurity – these might at least enable people to face God in the right frame of mind. Indeed, those who had never known poverty or deprivation or suffering might not know God as he really is. Misery perhaps gave a deeper understanding of God than plenty. In contrast, perhaps those who know all the answers (and can point to them in their bank balance) are really atheists at heart.

> Seek the Lord, all you *humble* of the land,
> who do his commands; seek righteousness, seek *humility;*
> perhaps you may be hidden
> on the day of the wrath of the Lord …
> I will leave in the midst of you a people *humble and lowly.*
> They shall seek refuge in the name of the Lord,
> those who are left in Israel …
> Sing aloud, O daughter of Zion …
> Rejoice and exult with all your heart …
> The King of Israel, the Lord, is in *your* midst …
> Do not fear, O Zion …
> The Lord your God is in *your* midst,
> a warrior who brings salvation.
> (Zephaniah 2:3, 3:12-17)

> This is the man to whom I [the Lord] will look:
> he that is *humble* and contrite in spirit,
> and trembles at my word.
> (Isaiah 66:2)

> I have uttered what I did not understand,
> things too wonderful for me,
> which I did not know ...
> I had heard of thee [God] by the hearing of the ear,
> but now my eye *sees* thee.
> (Job 42:3-5)

The quotation from Zephaniah is an important one. Zephaniah was the first to give a positive meaning to the word *anawim* – the lowly, humble and poor, whom he sees as the true people of God, the faithful remnant who alone will be able to survive future trials. The word is taken up in the quotation from the book of Isaiah, which identifies such people as God's favourites. The book of Psalms consistently does the same. Job too, the classic example of innocent suffering, testifies that it is only through his suffering that he now 'sees' God as he really is; before that, his hearsay knowledge of God was a misunderstanding. It is worth noting that Zephaniah envisages God as being in the midst (literally 'in the womb') of such *anawim*. Luke's Gospel will make much of this.

The understanding of God being proposed in these texts is not a mere minor adjustment of the understanding proposed earlier. It is in the strongest possible disagreement with it. There, poverty and misfortune were to be avoided like the plague, and God's help to do so was guaranteed. Here, poverty and misfortune are not to be avoided at all, because without them one might miss God. Suffering remains a tragedy, and unmerited suffering a dark mystery. But in the experience of suffering, God is not absent, he is more present than ever.

In other words, godliness requires a certain nakedness and

vulnerability. Where all is peace and security, the search for God as he really is has stopped. Those with vested interests feel very threatened by this message. Those with nothing to lose recognise it as news that is really good.

To put it bluntly, people tend to say, 'What a pity about the poor'. These texts say, 'What a pity about the rich!'

## Poverty in the Gospel

Just as the Old Testament's negative attitude towards poverty is echoed in the New, so also is this positive attitude. Luke, in particular, has appreciated the profound insights of the prophets, and is anxious to commend them to his readers. For him, Jesus is the typical Poor Man, with nowhere to lay his head, born in poverty and dying among the outcast. According to some Old Testament thinking, this should have made him God's reject. On the contrary, says Luke, it showed him to be closer to God than any other human being. In fact, he picks up Zephaniah's vision of God present in the midst of such poverty, and says it was fulfilled in Jesus:

| Zephaniah 3:14-20 | Luke 1:28-48 |
|---|---|
| Rejoice… | Rejoice |
| poor daughter of Jerusalem | (Mary in your 'lowliness')… |
| Do not fear… | Do not be afraid |
| for God rejoices over you… | for you have found favour with God |
| The Lord is in your midst (in your womb) | The Lord is with you… You will conceive in your womb and bear a son… |
| a warrior who brings salvation… | Jesus (the Lord brings salvation) |
| I will make you renowned among all the peoples of the earth. | Henceforth all generations will call me blessed. |

The state of godly poverty is here applied both to Jesus and to his mother. Her *Magnificat* does more than call for a revolution: it is a song in praise of poverty. It is because God has shown regard for his servant in her nothingness that all ages will call her blessed. Indeed, it is only those who acknowledge their nothingness whom God can help. How can we recognise that everything we have is a gift from God if our hands are not empty?

But it is not only Luke who speaks this language. Matthew, in a famous line, describes Jesus as 'meek and lowly of heart', classifying him as one of the *anawim*. And it is Matthew who sees the ideal followers of Jesus as belonging to the same blessed company: 'Blessed are the poor, the meek, the lowly, the humble, the sorrowful, the hungry, the persecuted' (Matthew 5:3-10). It is not that there is anything beautiful about being downtrodden, as if it might be helpful to tread on people in the belief that it will do them good. It is simply that suffering is no longer seen as an unmitigated disaster. It can be (though it will not always be) a road which leads more deeply into the mystery of God. And when it does, then those who suffer are indeed blessed. Theirs is the Kingdom. There is some sort of affinity between affliction and the Gospel which ought to make people stand in awe.

## Beggars before God

On one of my visits to the Holy Land, I took a group of pilgrims to look over the Ecumenical Institute at Tantur, near Bethlehem. Beyond the barbed wire fence that marks its perimeter, there was a stone shack inhabited by an Arab woman whose husband was killed by a landmine while he was grazing his sheep some years ago. The shack was so small that she had to do her cooking on an open fire in front of the entrance. One of the research students at the Institute came to consult the Rector about her thesis, which was entitled

'Blessed are the Poor'. The Rector suggested she might go and ask the widow if she had any ideas on the subject.

We must not get any sentimental ideas about poverty and deprivation. It is not an automatic door into heaven, and the poor and deprived will be the first to confirm that. In most respects, it should arouse our anger for its power to dehumanise people, and our pity and energy to fight against it.

On the other hand, we do not need to regard deprivation as a total disaster. In any sort of world, it could remind everyone that we all stand as beggars before God. And in the kind of world we live in, some degree of deprivation could actually help us understand God better. Because if God is the one who always rescues his chosen ones from suffering and pain, we clearly ought to do everything in our power to steer clear of suffering. But if God is the one who does not intervene to rescue six million Jews from the gas chambers, or tens of thousands of Christians from earthquakes, or Jesus himself from dying in near despair on the cross – then to suffer with these might enable us to come closer to that kind of God, who is the only kind of God that, as followers of Jesus, we should want to know. For in the pangs of suffering, God is not absent. He is more present than ever. And the Christian is called, like Mary, to give birth to such a God in our godforsaken world.

## Questions for discussion

- If different texts of the Bible can take diametrically opposed views on a subject such as poverty, how can we possibly discover God's own view?

- In what sense is the first of the Beatitudes ('Blessed are the poor') good news?

- Can the afflicted only be comforted by afflicting the comfortable?

# 2. On violence:
## *must a Christian be a pacifist?*

I remember reading a news item about a Northern Ireland 'supergrass' who admitted to so many murders that he was technically liable for 1762 years in prison. More recently, Iraq has claimed that the sanctions imposed upon the country by the West have been responsible for the death of half a million Iraqi children. In the USA, where he was finally tracked down, a high-ranking Nazi war criminal was charged with the death of 750,000 Yugoslavs.

The imagination can scarcely cope with such examples of violence. Yet they are echoed in the more 'homely' violence of which we read daily – bombings and terrorist attacks, muggings and rapes, child abuse and arson. Are we living in an increasingly violent world? Current events in Bosnia, Serbia, South America and Africa north, south, east and west, would seem to suggest so. Not to mention incidents on football pitches all over the world.

How should a Christian react to all this? How credible is 'praying for peace' in the light of such violent daily news items?

### *Who may exercise violence?*

Violence is a Latin word. It means using *vis* (force) against people or things. Violence is the violation of another, imposing one's own will forcefully over another. It means compelling someone to act against his or her will, or something to act against its nature. It means using pressure, whether physical (torture, bombs, and so on) or moral (blackmail, hostages, and the like) or psychological (fear, threats, etc.) to get one's own way.

How you react to violence will largely depend on which

33

side you identify with. It is a commonplace that one person's 'terrorist' is another's 'freedom fighter'. The same news item about troubles in Israel or Northern Ireland used to read like bad news to some, and like good news to others. When Ronald Reagan famously vowed to eliminate all terrorists, Fidel Castro asked, 'Who is being the terrorist now?'

Personally, I regularly exercise violence: over my garden, when I uproot the weeds I do not want, and 'force' the plants that I do; over the pieces of wood in my tool shed which I cut to my requirements and forcefully screw or nail together; over my beard when I daily destroy its natural growth; over my guitar when I tighten a piece of catgut to obtain a sound totally against the gut's nature; over myself and my environment when I over-eat or drive too fast; over my young children when I used to impose my will over theirs with a firm 'No!'

I am trying to establish the fact that violence, though the word is emotionally a strong one, is neither good nor bad. It is neutral. It is silly to talk of 'men of violence' when we all use violence in one way or another. 'Solutions must be found by discussion' sounds distinctly thin when said by people who colonised the world violently, and erected memorials everywhere to glorify that violence. To say 'All use of force is evil' is dishonest, especially when it is proclaimed by those churchmen who use spiritual blackmail to impose their views and refuse all discussion.

Which people are entitled to impose their will over against others? Well, presumably craftsmen are – gardeners and carpenters and others for the sake of the greater good which emerges from their use of violence (though our age is beginning to have second thoughts about respecting the environment). So also are parents and educators, whose firmness may not at the time be appreciated by their charges, but might be later on (though our age is more aware than past ages of the danger of child batterers and counterproductive teachers). And the approved 'authorities' are similarly so entitled, on behalf of those who approve of them – police, parliaments and popes (though our age is becoming more conscious of how easily such authorities may go beyond their brief). It goes without saying that those who approve of a police force must condone the violence these police exercise on behalf of those whom they protect.

## How should a Christian respond?

What does the Bible say about violence? What attitude does the Gospel commend Christians to take?

Many Christians imagine that they have no choice in the matter. Their reading of the New Testament tells them that the Gospel is totally opposed to violence: it commends resignation, tolerance, non-resistance, perhaps even pacifism. And they quote in corroboration the teaching of Jesus: to love all people, even enemies; to forgive those who trespass against us; to turn the other cheek; to walk the extra mile; to be reconciled with the brother before daring to offer gifts at the altar; to be the servant of others rather than lord it over them. Jesus beatified peacemakers, not bomb-throwers. He said, 'Whatever you do to the least of my brethren, you do to me', and 'He who takes up the sword will perish by the sword', meaning that violence only breeds counter-violence. He forbade Peter to defend him by violence, and himself gave the supreme example of non-violence by practising non-resistance to death. For his Kingdom is not of this world, and therefore cannot be promoted by this-worldly political means.

The position outlined above suggests that violence is not a Christian option. This viewpoint is taken by many. The words of Pope Leo XIII in the 1870s: 'In the last resort, Christians must endure injustice rather than rebel' – were echoed in the 1970s by Pope Paul VI: 'We have to affirm that violence is contrary to the Gospel, violence is not Christian', and by Pope John Paul II's action in demanding the resignation of the Nicaraguan priests who felt that the Gospel commanded them to enter politics. Malcolm Muggeridge regarded any involvement in politics in the name of Christ as an abominable blasphemy, and described the churches so involved as going 'on a sort of Gaderene jaunt', and the World Council of Churches as 'a group of men staggering home from the pub, their arms entwined, so that they will not fall over'.

## Selective

There is, however, more to be said. The selection of Gospel texts quoted above is very selective indeed, and does not do justice to the totality of Scripture.

To begin with, the whole story of the Old Testament is rooted in the concept of Holy War against the enemies of God, who must be exterminated, (and how other than violently?) in God's name. The earlier examples of this in the stories of the books of Exodus, Numbers and Joshua may embarrass us today, but we still warm to the stories of the Maccabee fight for freedom.

Christians may claim that their New Testament ethic rises above this level, with Jesus' command to love enemies. However, the opposite of love is not violence, but hatred, and it is presumably possible to offer resistance to enemies, even violently, without hating them. Certainly Christians have found no difficulty in continuing to wage war throughout their history, hopefully out of love for their enemies. And it was Christians who devised a whole theology of the 'Just War', laying down the conditions in which anger can be righteous, and the killing of a tyrant justified. Even the saintly Dietrich Bonhoeffer was involved in the plot to assassinate Hitler.

It is Christians, too, who have more recently devised a theology of liberation. This is based on recognising that there are three distinct kinds of violence, not just one. The media have made us very familiar with the violence of protests, strikes, and in extreme cases, armed struggle. But these are almost all cases of what may be called Violence II. Violence II is a secondary violence, and is a response to the more primary Violence I, where the system or structure is itself violent, where violence has become institutionalised.

It is not easy to recognise Violence I. If we are born into it and grow up within it, it becomes so much part of the scenery that we can remain unaware of it. But if it deprives people of their rights, if it oppresses and exploits and dehumanises them, then it is bound to blow up into the revolt that is Violence II. Which itself inevitably leads to the repression that is Violence III. 'It it those who make the peaceful revolution impossible,' J. F. Kennedy once warned, 'who make the violent revolution inevitable.' He was echoing the nineteenth century Irish agitator William O'Brien, who said, 'Violence is the only way of ensuring a hearing for moderation.' Even the gentle Martin Luther King said, 'A riot is the expression of a people who have not been listened to.'

In the past, Christians have too easily said, 'We should accept all our crosses as the will of God'. But surely what God wills is the liberation of people. Surely what God wants is for people to be freed from injustice, exploitation and oppression, from unemployment, hunger and disease, from a system in which basic human rights are denied them. And if that system has so fossilised that no amount of discussion can change it, it has to be destroyed. And if people have become so much a part of the system that they do not even notice how unjust it is, they too may have to have violence done to them if they are to be liberated. Few people in the northern hemisphere are aware that by keeping for ourselves what others basically need, we practise a form of violence against them. Few people anywhere are aware that when we see others only in terms of the advantage they can be to us, we do violence to them.

At Medellin, in 1968, the Latin American Roman Catholic bishops provided a kind of charter for Liberation theology. They stated:

> A minority of privileged people has practised violence against the vast majority of deprived people. It is the violence of hunger, helplessness and underdevelopment. It is the violence of persecution, oppression and neglect.

Archbishop Helder Camara added that when Violence II erupts in reaction to this, it is not only inevitable, but must be respected. Liberation theologians add that this is not only allowed by the Gospel: the Gospel commands it.

## *Some quotes:*

> The Christian who is not a revolutionary is living in mortal sin. *(Camillo Torres)*

> To all intents and purposes, it is today illegal to be an authentic Christian. Why? Because the world around is founded on an established disorder. To proclaim the Gospel against this disorder is subversive. *(Archbishop Oscar Romero)*

> Take the resistance fighters of occupied Europe, who used violence against their Nazi oppressors. We don't call them 'terrorists'. Why? Because we accept that their cause was just and their methods disciplined. If Christians refuse to condemn the use of violence in the attempt to end injustice, it is because they recognise that we have no right to condemn the use of violence by others in pursuit of justice if we are prepared to use it ourselves for the same end. *(Programme to Combat Racism, World Council of Churches 1977)*

Not all cases of conflict are the same. We can imagine a private quarrel between two people or groups whose differences are based upon misunderstandings. In such cases it would be appropriate to talk and negotiate to sort out the misunderstandings and to reconcile the two sides. But there are other conflicts in which one side is right and the other wrong. There are conflicts where one side is a fully armed and violent oppressor while the other side is defenceless and oppressed. There are conflicts that can only be described as the struggle between justice and injustice, good and evil, God and the devil. To speak of reconciling these two is not only a mistaken application of the Christian idea of reconciliation, it is a total betrayal of all that Christian faith has ever meant. Nowhere in the Bible or in Christian tradition has it ever been suggested that we ought to try to reconcile good and evil, God and the devil. We are supposed to do away with evil, injustice, oppression and sin – not come to terms with it. (*The Kairos Document*, a statement signed by 150 theologians in South Africa in 1985.)

I am opposed to all forms of violence … But I am aware, as a man of peace, that there may come a time … when we will have to say that the lesser of the two evils is to overthrow this unjust system. *(Archbishop Desmond Tutu, 1985)*

Christian society in Britain has domesticated the Gospel. It is geared to loving God in moderation. We may give alms to the poor, visit the sick and the lonely, hold annual bazaars and flag days for those in need – in fact do any good works which do not threaten the pattern of our society. But to demand justice at the expense of people's comfort or security – that makes us troublemakers. *(Dr Sheila Cassidy)*

What would the Good Samaritan have done if his donkey had gone faster and arrived on the scene sooner? Should he have reined in his animal and waited on the other side of the road until the robbers had finished beating the poor man and taken off with their spoils? Or should he have waded into the fight and tried to beat the robbers off with his whip? Surely there are circumstances in which it is not only the right, but the duty of the Christian to use counter-violence against unjust violence.

There is even a further possibility. Suppose that the Good Samaritan passed the same way every week, and nearly every time found someone who had been beaten up and robbed. Would he fulfil his Christian duty simply by binding up the wounds of each and taking them to hospital at his expense? Rather, would he not have to recognise that he was dealing, not with casual violence, but with institutionalised violence, and – while helping the victims – concentrate his major effort on finding and eliminating the source? (From Gary MacEoin's *Memoirs and Memories*, 1986)

'When King Herod heard this, he was perturbed,
and so was the whole of Jerusalem.'
Herod had a right to be perturbed.
So does every Herod who sits on a throne of his people's bones,
and drinks his people's tears as unrighteous wine.
For coming to birth in Jerusalem
is a new Future for those on the margins of power.
The old arrangement will be no more,
and the One who whispered in Abraham's ear
and flared in Moses' face
will once more pull down the mighty from their thrones.
The baby's helplessness will prove stronger,
and Herod will be declared NO-KING.
The madonna's smile signifies something
only understood in Israel's blood.
Soon the hungry will be filled with all good things.
Scream, rage and weep – 'no-kings', wherever you sit,
El Salvador, Guatemala, Pretoria, Moscow, Washington.
Jesus comes, and through us will build
God's kingdom of peace and justice.
*(from a Christmas card sent by a friend)*

### Turbulent priests

Fighting words! And highly political words too. As was pointed out earlier, some Christians find such talk highly disturbing, and label it the 'social Gospel', which has lost all contact with the 'spiritual Gospel' of the New Testament.

But if the New Testament proclaims that God is incarnate in the lives of people, how can the Gospel be anything other than social? If politics is concerned with improving relationships between people, how can Christianity (or indeed any other religion) avoid being political? Many Christian missionaries, working among the poor and oppressed, with the highest spiritual motives, are beginning to declare that they find it impossible to remain politically uninvolved, however virulently they are accused of being 'turbulent priests'. Many nuns and Christian lay people say the same.

In short, many Christians, and their number is growing, have become convinced that fighting words are not only compatible with the Gospel, but are the very heart of it. They maintain that until we read the Bible through the eyes of the marginalised, we fail to read it as Jesus read it. The Church, such as he envisaged it, is *identified* with the poor and underprivileged. A Church which only stands *alongside* the poor, or thinks of itself as having only a mission *to* the poor from on high, or (worse) is aligned with the class that continues to oppress the poor – this is no longer the Church of Christ. Christianity is nothing if it does not make a 'preferential option' *for* the poor, and relentlessly champion their cause. 'He's sent me to proclaim good news to the poor,' Jesus proclaimed in his first sermon in Nazareth, 'to set the downtrodden free' (Luke 4:18).

### Options

Which side will we opt for? Which interpretation of the Gospel will we make our own, the 'spiritual' one or the 'political' one?

It is easy to have double standards and to opt for both, at different times. When justice is being flagrantly violated, we shout enthusiastically for action to be taken, even violently, and applaud loudly any success such action may have, whether it be in Kosovo or Afghanistan, in Africa or Central America. Self-determination, self-expression, freedom – these are uppermost in our mind.

But when this kind of action threatens our own interests, then stability, order and respect for law tend to take priority even over justice, and the erstwhile 'freedom-fighter' is easily labelled 'terrorist', whether it be in Northern Ireland or Israel, on a hijacked plane or in a riot-torn suburb. In such cases, the *status quo* is readily thought to have the sole right to exercise violence.

Which side does the Gospel opt for? Or does that too adopt different standards at different times? Certainly it is centred on a figure who absorbs trouble rather than taking up arms against it. The cross is a powerful symbol of suffering passivity, of the ineffective victim whose sheer dignity is more powerful even than the violence of his torturers.

But the Gospel does not only issue a command to personal and private godliness. It issues a challenge to public values too, and these may be so deep-rooted that no amount of merely private conversions can change them. They may require the subversion of society. They certainly call for political praxis rather than mere theory. Even the beautiful *Magnificat* is an open invitation to revolution.

The Gospel leaves us the right to choose which of the two aspects we will stress. It does not speak with a single voice. Even the world eventually approves of violent revolutions, once they have proved successful.

## *Questions for Discussion*

- Who, in your opinion, is entitled to impose his or her will over others?

- Which Gospel texts speak more loudly to you – those which commend toleration and peacefulness, or those which urge resistance to injustice and the liberation of the oppressed?

- How do you react to the re-telling of the parable of the Good Samaritan on pages 39-40?

# 3. On peace: *rest or unrest?*

Christians find it quite natural to associate the word 'peace' with Jesus. His birth story in the Gospel is greeted with a song of glory in heaven and 'peace on earth'. His healing ministry is punctuated with the command to 'go in peace'. With his friends in particular he is lavish with the word: 'My peace I give to you, my peace I leave with you.' And this is especially true of the risen Christ, whose 'Peace be with you' becomes a kind of refrain. St Paul adopted the word for the regular greeting with which he opened his letters: 'Grace be to you, and peace.' And so the word entered the Christian liturgy, with the invitation at Communion time to give each other a sign of peace: 'May the peace of the Lord be always with you.'

In the light of all these references, it comes as a bit of a surprise to find Jesus saying, according to Matthew 10:34: 'Do not think that I have come to bring peace on earth; I have not come to bring peace, but a sword.' Obviously, the term 'Peace of Christ' is ambiguous. We need some clarification.

## Shalom

We may find some insight by analysing the Hebrew word which Jesus would actually have used – *shalom*. The word (or its Arabic equivalent *salaam*) is still used throughout the Middle East today as a greeting when people meet or leave each other. It means more than our 'hello' and 'goodbye'. It means, literally, 'Peace be with you'.

But it also means more than a westerner might mean in saying, 'Peace be with you'. The western concept of peace is fairly negative, having been inherited from the Greeks, whose word *eirene* means no more than the opposite of enmity. 'Peace' for a Greek meant the end of hostilities, ceasefire, armistice. And all westerners tend to use the word 'peace' in the same negative sense.

When we pray for peace in Northern Ireland or in the Balkans, our main concern is that the struggle will stop. When we hope for industrial peace, we yearn for an end to strikes and disputes. When we say, 'Oh for a bit of peace!' we are longing for the noise and turmoil to end and for quiet to take over. If we said, 'Peace be with you', as we left our friends, it would mean no more than 'I hope no trouble comes your way'. And when we put 'Rest in Peace' on tomb-stones, we envisage an eternity of glorious inactivity after a lifetime of hassle. Christian life is a struggle: peace only comes later.

> Now the labourer's task is o'er,
> now the battle day is past …
> There no more the powers of hell
> can prevail to mar their peace.
> (J. Ellerton)

> Jerusalem, my happy home,
> name ever dear to me!
> When shall my labours have an end,
> in joy, and peace, and thee?
> (J. Bromehead)

> Jesu, in mercy bring us
> to that dear land of rest …
> O happy retribution!
> Short toil, eternal rest …
> (Bernard of Cluny, tr. J. M. Neale)

> It is enough: earth's struggles soon shall cease,
> and Jesus call us to heaven's perfect peace.
> (E. H. Bickersteth)

O may this bounteous God
through all our life be near us,
with ever joyful hearts
and blessed peace to cheer us;
and keep us in his grace,
and guide us when perplexed,
and free us from all ills
in this world and the next.
(M. Rinkart, tr. C. Winkworth)

The last words she said were, 'Dear friends, I am going
where washing ain't wanted, nor mending, nor sewing,
where all things is done just exact to my wishes,
where folk never eat, and there's no washing dishes…
Don't mourn for me now, don't mourn for me never;
I'm going to nothing for ever and ever.'
(Anonymous, 19th century)

The Hebrew word *shalom* is not negative like that. It is a very positive word. It is rooted in a word meaning 'completeness'. When people, or things, or situations, have all the ingredients for making them what they should be, with nothing missing, then you apply the word *shalom*, not before. *Shalom* is totality, wholeness, fullness, maturity. Its opposite is not 'trouble', but 'handicap'.

*Shalom* means entirely integrated, complete, head to foot, top to bottom, in and out, up to the brim, every inch. *Shalom* means happiness, not in the sense of the blissful grin that a bottle of whisky can bring, but in the sense of well-being, health and ability to cope. *Shalom* means harmony, first with oneself in the sense of being totally in control and not in fits and starts. But then also with one's neighbours, and with the rest of the human race. And finally with nature, and with God. In short, *shalom* means being fully alive, fully at work, fully operating, complete.

The image that is conjured up by the word *shalom*, therefore, is not of corpses covered with wreaths of flowers resting in 'peace'; but of people in their prime, vibrant and in command of all their faculties. The picture that one has to have in mind is not of an engine that is now switched off, dead and inactive, but of a machine running so smoothly that all that can be heard is the hum. Or of an orchestra in which all the players are meticulously playing their own individual part, but in perfect harmony. That is *shalom*.

## Enemies of 'shalom'

The world that God planned and created was one that was to enjoy a state of *shalom*. When the Bible wanted to express this conviction pictorially, it spoke of God's battle with a monster called Chaos, and his victory over it. The *shalom* that ensued, as was pointed out above, is envisaged not as a mere cessation of hostilities with this enemy, but as its destruction. And since it is Chaos that has been overcome, the story presents God's planned world as one that is well and filled with activity, yet in total harmony.

In keeping with that picture, anything which threatens such a world is evil, and must be resisted at all costs. Any misfortune – deprivation, suffering, injustice, exploitation. Or any handicap – physical or mental. Or any shortcomings which interfere with the world's wellbeing – plumbing which won't work, cars which break down, dry rot. Or any disturbance of life's harmony – quarrelsomeness, hatred, enmity. Or any threat to life's fullness – an early death, even a late death. All these are envisaged as barriers to the harmony, fullness, completeness and wellbeing that God bequeathed on his creation.

Most terrible of all, more loathsome than all the misfortunes listed above, is the toleration of them, the suggestion that they do not matter. To connive at evil, or even to take evil lightly, whether it be sickness or handicap or death – this is to let the chaotic floodwaters sweep back over God's creation and destroy it. It does not merely 'disturb the peace' when all we are looking for is a quiet life. It actually undermines the world that God has made, undoing the work of creation and turning God's work upside down. It is in these terms that the psalmist turns in anger on the magistrates of his day who have perverted justice:

> Your task was to rescue the needy,
> to give their rights to the poor,
> to defend the defenceless in prison,
> and throw wide open their door.

> But no! You've lost all your senses,
> your finer feelings are dead,
> you wander about in your darkness,
> you have stood the world on its head!
> (Psalm 82:3-5, tr. H. J. Richards)

In short, there can be no *shalom* while there is injustice, or the toleration of it. The fundamental opposite of *shalom* is not war, as it is for our westernised 'peace'. The opposite of *shalom* is injustice. The book of Isaiah puts it memorably in the lovely Christmas reading of chapter 11, linking peace and harmony with justice and equity; and even more succinctly in chapter 57:21: 'There is no *shalom* says my God, for the wicked.' This is often said, with a self-deprecating smile, by the busy. But its meaning is more serious. While wickedness abounds, peace is illusory, a sham.

## Genuine and false 'shalom'

It is in this wide context that we have to think again about the reported words of Jesus: 'Do you think that I have come to give peace on earth?' (Luke 12:51); 'My peace I give to you – but not as the world gives' (John 14:27).

The words can easily be misinterpreted. Our first reaction

is to imagine that Jesus is deprecating mere worldly harmony, and setting our minds on an other-worldly peace. But as we have seen, an easterner would never make such a strange distinction. If God made the world *shalom,* then it is the *shalom* of this world that we have to preserve, not that of some other imaginary world. We naturally turn to otherworldly language to insist that the values we are concerned about are transcendent, that they lie deep and not on the surface. But the values we are talking about are here and now, not in some *post-mortem* existence. If God made the world good, it is blasphemy to depreciate the world, or to be suspicious of it, or to opt out of it. The Jewish Talmud puts it in these terms: 'Come the Judgement, we will be held to account for every worldly pleasure we have failed to enjoy.' Good is good, whether it is spiritual or material.

But there is a real good and an illusory one. There is a genuine harmonious completeness and a superficial one. If people say *'shalom',* when deep down there is nothing but chaos, a curse on them!

And so Jesus says, 'Peace? It depends what you mean. Peace to you, my friends, certainly. But don't imagine that means "peace and quiet". My peace means trouble.' A superficial peace that does not deal with the underlying chaos is a sham. The prophet, even though he represents the peace of God, must often take on the role of Troubler of Israel.

I came to set the world on fire –
how I wish the fire were burning now!
Mine is a dangerous life;
how hard it will be for me until the work is done!
Do you think it is 'peace' I have come to give the world?
I tell you No – the very opposite of 'peace'!
(Luke 12:49-51, tr. A. T. Dale)

To insist that peace should be built on real justice is to ask for a baptism of fire. In the kind of world we live in, the peace of Christ will often feel like a sword.

What then, is the genuine *shalom* of Christ? It is the harmony which God intended the whole of creation to enjoy. It is a fullness of life lived in this world, with all its good things seen as a gift, not as a threat. It is exemplified in the man Jesus, whom the New Testament sees, particularly in his risen glory, as a second Adam presiding over a new creation. It is not achieved without blood.

## Destructiveness and healing

We have been speaking as if the only threat to peace lay in the institutions against which Jesus battled, and which are perpetuated in our world, even by Christians. But of course it is not only the establishment that endangers our peace.

The famous fable of the Scorpion and the Fish, puts the point neatly. A scorpion on its travels comes to a river it cannot cross. It calls out to a fish to give it a lift. 'Don't be silly,' says the fish. 'Halfway across you'd raise your sting and kill me.' 'Don't be silly,' replies the scorpion. 'If I killed you, I'd go to the bottom with you.' Impressed by the logic, the fish says, 'Jump on.' Sure enough, as they get halfway, the scorpion raises its tail and stings the fish. With its dying breath, the fish asks, 'Why did you do it?' 'I don't know,' replies the drowning scorpion. 'It's in my nature.'

The chaos that threatens our peace lies deep in the heart of each of us, as part of our nature. Each of us carries a well of destructiveness, and it is so much part of us that we draw from it without thinking, even if it is the death of us.

But there is also the famous story of Ibrahim and Yussef. Both had a camel-load of goods to be sold in Damascus. As they prepared to set off, Ibrahim's mother fell sick, so Yussef offered to take both camels, assuring his friend that he would take the same loving care of his camel as of his own. A week passed, with Ibrahim anxiously scanning the horizon.

Eventually he spied Yussef leading back two empty camels, one of which was thinner and wearier than the other. 'What happened?'

'I don't know. I treated them both the same. They both had the same food and water. It's just that at night, when I slept between the two camels, I put my head closer to mine than to yours.'

If the first fable is true, is it not good news that the second story is also true? In spite of the well of destructiveness that each of us carries, we also each possess a healing force to which even camels respond. And this force is able at all times to restore the harmonious *shalom* which God intends his creation to enjoy.

## Questions for Discussion

- 'While wickedness abounds, peace is a sham' (Isaiah 57:21). Suggest some examples.

- Who are the really peaceful people you know? On what is this peace based?

- Is 'peace' the word you most naturally associate with Jesus? Explain why, or why not.

# 4. On worldliness:
## *out of this world or in it?*

### *What do I treasure?*

Right up to the time he was four years old, my son Pedro had an overwhelming affection for a rather grubby hand puppet, known as Bertie Badger, first given him when he was aged one. Whenever he was upset, or hurt, or just tired, he 'needed' Bertie Badger. Nothing else would do. It was the treasure that totally satisfied him. It was his consolation and peace.

I sometimes wonder if, when all the cards are finally down, the things I personally hold dear will seem as pathetic. What in my life do I hold most dear? What do I prize and value most highly? What ought I to treasure?

My childhood catechism gave me a very clear answer:

Q. Of which must you take more care, your body or your soul?

A. I must take more care of my soul, for Christ said, 'What doth it profit a man if he gain the whole world, and suffer the loss of his own soul?'

Q. Why did God make you?

A. God made me to know him, love him, and serve him in this world, and to be happy with him for ever in the next.

Happiness, contentment, fulfilment – these would come later. Here and now it was service and hard slog. The reward would come in the next world. Our treasure is elsewhere, not here.

## *Otherworldliness*

At first glance, those neat catechism answers seem to put in a nutshell the content of a whole number of New Testament texts. The quotations are famous: the Sermon on the Mount, where Jesus counsels his audience not to lay up treasures for themselves on earth, 'where moth and rust consume and where thieves break in and steal, but lay up for yourselves treasures in heaven,' where they will be immune to moths and burglars. 'Where your treasure is, there will your heart be also' (Matthew 6:19-21). Luke tells the story of the Rich Fool, who builds larger and larger barns to store the grain that is going to featherbed his retirement. 'Fool!' God says to him. 'This night your soul is required of you; and the things you have prepared, whose will they be?' Has he been rich toward God? (Luke 12:16-21.) A few chapters further on, the Rich Ruler is described as the really poor man, because he cannot bring himself to share his wealth with the poor, and so misses the Kingdom of God (Luke 18:18-30). There are some cuttingly negative references to 'the world' both by John (for whom worldliness is the very opposite of godliness, in 1 John 2:15), and by Paul (who advises sitting very loosely to something as transient as the world, in 1 Corinthians 7:31). But the most brilliant word picture fills the closing pages of the New Testament, where the fall of affluent Rome is eagerly anticipated, to the dismay of all the merchant navies of the ancient world, for whom Rome was the market:

No one buys their cargo any more,
cargo of gold, silver, jewels and pearls,
fine linen, purple, silk and scarlet,
all kinds of scented wood, all articles of ivory,
all articles of costly wood, bronze, iron and marble,
cinnamon, spice, incense, myrrh, frankincense,
wine, oil, fine flour and wheat,
cattle and sheep, horses and chariots – and slaves …

Alas, alas, for the great city
that was clothed in fine linen, in purple and scarlet,
bedecked with gold, with jewels, and with pearls!
In one hour, all this wealth has been laid waste.
(Revelation 18:11-17)

The note that sounds throughout these texts, of mistrust of earthly treasures and even contempt for them, is strongly echoed in the Christian liturgy, which urges God to:

teach us to despise earthly things, and to desire only the things of heaven.
(Prayer after Communion, Second Sunday of Advent)

The real world is the world to come. This world is only a shadow, and has no importance or value of its own, except as a testing place for the next world. There is no point even in trying to change the world: that would be as useless as changing one earthly currency into another, when the only currency we will eventually need is a heavenly one. Real life begins only when this life has ended. The meaning of our life is to give no meaning to our life, only to our after-life. That is where our real treasure lies.

No one has expressed this viewpoint more pungently than the poet John Donne, in one of his funeral elegies:

Think that no stubborne sullen Anchorit,
Which fixt to a pillar, or a grave, doth sit
Bedded, and bath'd in all his ordures, dwels
So fowly as our Soules in their first-built Cels.
*(An Anatomie of the World)*

St Teresa of Avila put it more succinctly:

Life on earth is only a single night we spend in a second-class hotel.

Most pithily, the wisecrack:

Serve the Lord; the pay isn't much, but the retirement benefits are out of this world.

## God so loved the world

'Out of this world.' A desire to escape from this world. A contempt for this world as a sleazy overnight hotel. A disdain for the bodies which tie us down to this world, contaminating our souls like a dung heap. Is this really the heart of a Christianity which preaches that God so loved the world that he gave his only Son to save it, and that the human body is the temple of the Holy Spirit? Surely not. Surely there has been some misunderstanding here.

Certainly, such a world-denying attitude is the very antithesis of the Old Testament – and Jesus was brought up on the Old Testament. For the Jews – and Jesus was a Jew – the world was not a vale of tears, but the very place where God is revealed. The body was not something to be crushed, but something to be treasured and cared for until it too became a revelation of God. What the Jews of the Old Testament yearned for was not life after death, but life after life after life, because life is of God. What they most treasured was not their own individual union with God, but the reconciliation with God of all their brothers and sisters, indeed of all God's marvellous creation. How could anyone revel in his own salvation while anything remained unsaved?

And so religion, for the Jews, was not about abdicating from this world, but about taking responsibility for it; not about saving their own skin, but about giving their life away in the way that God does. Religion was not about souls imprisoned in bodies, but about bodies marvellously endowed with souls; not about a heaven beyond the skies, but about the earth down here, and the people that live in it. The tense they used to describe the meeting of men and women with God was not the future but the present, not the hereafter but the here and now.

It is interesting to compare some of our world-denying spirituality with the robust hopes of the Jewish prophet, who looks forward to a future when:

> on this mountain [Zion]
> the Lord of hosts will make for all peoples
> a feast of fat things,
> a feast of wine on the lees,
> of fat things full of marrow,
> of wine on the lees well refined
> (Isaiah 25:6-7)

## *The preaching of Jesus*

We have considered some New Testament texts above. Here is a further selection, which perhaps expresses the good news at the heart of Jesus' preaching better than those others.

What Jesus preaches is not the Kingdom of 'heaven', but the Kingdom of 'The Heavens' – a polite Jewish title for God. And that Kingdom of God, he says, 'is in your midst, among people, here and now' (Luke 17:21). What he hands over to Peter, therefore, is not the keys of a future heaven, but the keys which open the doors of that present Kingdom of God (Matthew 16:19). For his prayer is that God's will may be done on earth, not somewhere else (Matthew 6:10).

People, therefore, are at the centre of the good news he preaches. They come first. The sabbath is made for people, not vice versa (Mark 2:27), and the same is presumably true of any other sacred institution – churches, shrines, liturgy, sacraments, prayer books, ministry, monasteries, Canterburys and Vaticans. The care of parents is a finer worship of God than the keeping of religious laws (Mark 7:11). Reconciliation with brothers and sisters is more important than offering gifts in church, and those who remain unreconciled are not to put anything in the plate (Matthew 5:23). What God asks of people is not sacrifice ('doing a sacred thing') but ordinary secular things like mercy, compassion and justice for all (Matthew 9:13); because what divides people into sheep and goats, in the last analysis, is simply the way they treat each other, and judgement will be passed on no other grounds (Matthew 25:31-46). It is where two or three are gathered together that God is present, and it is this reality that should command our worship (Matthew 18:20).

In the light of these Gospel texts, it is not surprising that the rest of the New Testament speaks of the ordinary human followers of Jesus as the 'Body of Christ'. It is in that everyday secular reality that Christ continues to be embodied in the world. So Jesus can be portrayed as praying that his followers, while remaining rooted in the world, may be with him where he is – totally at one with God (John 17:24). In New Testament language, 'eternal life' is not a heavenly reward reserved for the indefinite future: it is a reality available here and now, in the present tense, as John keeps repeating:

> God gave his only Son that whoever believes in him should [now] *have* eternal life (John 3:16).
>
> He who believes in the Son *has* eternal life (John 3:36).
>
> The bread of God is that which comes down from heaven, and *gives* life to the world (John 6:33).
>
> He who believes *has* eternal life (John 6:47).
>
> He who eats my flesh and drinks my blood *has* eternal life (John 6:54).
>
> I came that they may [here and now] *have* life (John 10:10).
>
> My sheep hear my voice … and I *give* them eternal life (John 10:27-28).
>
> I *am* the resurrection and the life (John 11:25).
>
> This *is* eternal life, that they know thee the only true God (John 17:3).

These are written that you may… *have* life in his name (John 20:31).

God gave us eternal life, and this life is in his Son. He who has the Son *has* life (1 John 5:11-12)

One text puts these in a nutshell:

I came to help people to live – and to live splendidly. (John 10:10 tr. A. T. Dale)

## *Metaphors*

If all these texts put so much emphasis on the present, on this world and on the earth, how can we reconcile them with those earlier texts which emphasised the future, the other world and heaven? If the message of Jesus concerns our life in this world, how do we interpret talk of the 'other world'?

By putting it into inverted commas. By speaking of an 'as if'. By realising that we are using a metaphor or a second language, because our ordinary everyday language is inadequate, and cannot properly express what needs to be said. The two languages, since they are picture languages, suggest that we are talking of two storeys, an upstairs and a downstairs. In actual fact they are no more than two 'stories' about the same reality.

When we use the second language, the world that is being renounced is not the world as such, as if we wanted it to stop so that we could get off. We are talking about the surface world, the superficial world, the shallow and trivial world which can never satisfy human yearnings. And the 'heaven' that is being yearned for is not to be found somewhere else, but in the deep things of life, in what is profound and ultimately satisfying. In this language, the command not to lay up treasures for ourselves 'on earth' is simply a striking way of saying: 'Do not opt for what is immediately and superficially attractive. Your capacity is infinite, and your hearts will be restless until they embrace the infinite.' But that transcendent reality is not to be found somewhere else. The infinite, the deep, the profound – these have to be found in our own lives, on earth, in our world. For Christians, like Jews, are committed to 'incarnation'. They may not, like other people, keep pointing away from the world, as if all the real and worthwhile things lie outside. They are committed to the belief that God is to be found *in carne* and not outside it, in human history and human flesh, however incredible this may sound.

## Deep things

What, then, are the deep things in our lives, the treasure that we should most cherish? In a famous line, St Paul refers to the treasure being carried in 'earthen vessels', that is to say, in fragile pots, to be handled with care (2 Corinthians 4:7). The description is not meant to be an apology, as if the treasure should be ashamed of its poor packaging. Human nature is indeed fragile, but it is all the packaging that there is, and if the treasure is not presented in that package, it is not presented at all. And what finally is the treasure? The preceding verse specifies it: it is the glory of God, as revealed in the face of Christ, shining into our hearts.

The ultimate treasure, needless to say, is God: that is what people mean when they use the word 'God'. This God, of course, lies beyond all imagination or thinking: by definition, God is the ultimate mystery. But there is one clue to that impenetrable mystery, Paul is saying, and it is the utterly human face of a member of the human race, Jesus of Nazareth.

Those who want to know the unknowable God must gaze into the face of this man. And when they see, in his life and teaching and death, someone who lives for others, someone who gives himself away, someone who can ultimately only be defined in terms of acceptance, forgiveness, mercy and love – then they will know what God is like. And if their heart's desire is to be at one with that God, then they cannot do anything other than walk in the footsteps of Jesus.

The Christian must treasure anything that is Christlike, for that is true godliness. Wherever there is love, God is there. All those who live in love, live in God, and God lives in them, whether they call themselves Christians, or Muslims or atheists.

In that context, perhaps Pedro's puppet was not such a bad image of what ought to be treasured. When he pulled Bertie Badger close and hugged him, he was showing some sort of love. It was little enough, heaven knows, and he has gradually had to learn how much more love can ultimately demand of him. But at his four-year-old level, he was showing love, and if that is what the word 'God' is all about, he had found his true treasure. He was at least beginning to put his heart where his treasure is.

## Questions for Discussion

- An 'otherworldly' Christianity is repudiated by many Christians today as a dangerous deviation from the good news of the Gospel. What are the dangers in a thoroughly 'worldly' understanding of Christianity?

- By definition, Christianity is about the incarnation of the otherworldly in the worldly. To what extent has the history of Christianity displayed or hidden this truth?

- Is a religion in which 'the worldly' means no more than the superficial, and 'the heavenly' means no more than the profound, worthwhile?

# 5. On providence:
## *divine plan or divine presence?*

St Paul, writing to the Christians in Rome, makes a very bold statement, which it would be worth unravelling:

> To them that love God, all things work together for good. (Romans 8:28)

It must take a great deal of faith to make such an assertion. That all things, all circumstances, all the ups and downs of my life, all the people I meet, all the things that happen to me – that these form some great divine pattern – that needs a lot of believing.

### *Lack of faith*

Why do I say that? Because so much of our experience seems to contradict it. So much of my life seems haphazard, without any plan except the one I impose on it. Much of my life is utterly meaningless, and it would be silly to pretend it was part of a great plan. A good deal of my life is downright evil: not only the evil that I do personally, but the evil that lies totally outside my control – the natural disasters of which I read daily in the press, and the personal disasters of which I am made daily aware, of frustration, and loss, and handicap, and breakdown, and death. How can all this 'work together for [my] good'? Whether I love God or not, a great deal of it seems to be working together for my harm!

Paul's text seems to reply: That is because you have not yet seen the final result. The back of a piece of tapestry is all thread and knots and loose ends. But when it is turned around to show the right side, all the ugly bits make sense. It is impossible to make a tapestry without knots; the awkward bits are not some unfortunate mistake, they are essential. So even the suffering that people undergo is an essential part of the final overall pattern. Just be patient and wait till you see the result, and you will realise the meaning and purpose of it all. Because 'to them that love God, all things work together for good'.

Nor would it be difficult to find other biblical texts to back up this optimistic view of life. There are texts about the goodness of creation, and about a world which works for our good, not our harm. There are texts about the providence which protects and cherishes those who love God. There are texts about each hair of our head being numbered, and about each sparrow being precious in the eyes of God. And if we could not say Amen to texts like that, because personal experience had given us a far more sombre view of life, we would have to conclude that we lacked faith, and try to repeat St Paul's words like a holy Couéism, in the hope that we would acquire a more sanguine outlook: 'To them that love God, all things *do* work together for good.'

## *The best of all possible worlds?*

A cynic has defined optimists as those who believe we live in the best of all possible worlds, and pessimists as those who are afraid this may be true. In other words, if the optimistic view we have analysed above is the true one, then we are in real trouble! Some people may succeed in painting a rosy picture of the world, but in reality it is a fairly fearsome place to live in. And if it has been planned that way, if it is not simply one of several worlds God might have made but the best he could manage, then one would have to say to God, as George Bernard Shaw wanted to, 'Surely you could have done better than this?'

After reading the daily papers, or listening to the television news, who goes to bed feeling that 'God's in his heaven and all's right with the world'? Would it not be more honest to admit that the universe is not an orderly system in which everything will come right in the end? More honest to acknowledge that it is in fact a very twisted system, in which everything that can go wrong will do so unless we stop it? More reasonable to recognise that if things do happily go our way – we got the job we wanted, we had fine weather for the fête, we missed the plane that crashed, we won some money on the Lottery – this is not a special providence of a God who loves me more than other people, but sheer chance?

The parishioners of a small town in Peru have been 'adopted' by the parish to which I belong in England. They wrote to tell us of the seven years of drought they have had to endure, and asked us to join with them in praying for rain. We did so with enthusiasm, and the rains came. And came. And came. The town was declared a disaster area as floods turned adobe houses into mud, undermined the roads, swept bridges away, and washed all the arable land into the river. What sort of providence is this?

When Israel built the monument of Yad Vashem outside Jerusalem, it was to keep a permanent record of the World War II horrors, which many would have preferred to forget: the successful extermination of six million Jews in a programme that hoped eventually to eliminate Jewry throughout the world; the mass graves; the mountains of spectacles and rings and false teeth that were being saved for the 'war effort'; the officer in charge of the massacre at Babi Yar going home to sing Christmas carols round the crib with his children. No wonder a lot of Jews are frightened of us Christians! What sort of a God is it that could plan a world like that? What sort of a blasphemy is it that suggests it is all working together for good, or that can speak of the good that emerges as outweighing such an obscenity?

Nothing can ever compensate for the suffering of the innocent. A God who needs the suffering of the innocent as the knots behind his tapestry is a monster, and most people feel incapable of worshipping a God of that kind. All things do not work together for good. Whether we love God or ignore him, a great deal of our experience tells us that many things work together for our harm. It is sheer naïveté to say, 'Have faith, it's all for your good.'

## The Bible

There is, of course, plenty of biblical warrant for this more sombre world-view. A splendid modern prayer book offers these one-line meditations:

> Last night, Lord, I dreamt I made a world, and put *You* in it.

> Lord, thanks for telling me You love me. I would never have guessed.

> Dear God, if You're thinking of providing for me today like you did yesterday, forget it.

> Lord, despair is the nicest thing that ever happened to me, because now I'm never disappointed.

> (P. De Rosa, *Prayers for Pagans and Hypocrites*, London 1989)

We smile at such impudent words. But they are no more than an echo of many pages of the Old Testament. Both Ecclesiastes and Job protest in the strongest terms that life is not a bed of roses but more like a crown of thorns, and that it is difficult to get any meaning out of it, if indeed there is one. Many of the psalms confess that the presence of God most often feels like his absence, and that the God who palpably protects those who believe in him simply does not exist. Worse, the hidden God who does exist feels very much like no God at all! Many of the prophets found their close relationship with God not a joy, but an anguish, and did not hesitate to say so:

> O Lord, thou hast deceived me,
> and I was deceived;
> thou art stronger than I,
> and thou hast prevailed.
> I have become a laughing stock all the day;
> everyone mocks me.
> For whenever I speak, I cry out,
> I shout, 'Violence and destruction!'
> For the word of the Lord has become for me
> a reproach and derision all day long.
> If I say, 'I will not mention him,
> or speak any more in his name,'
> there is in my heart as it were a burning fire
> shut up in my bones,
> and I am weary with holding it in,
> and I cannot.
> (Jeremiah 20:7-9)

For a man like Jeremiah, even though he loved God more than most, all things did not work together for good. Nor did he pretend that they did. Singing in the rain he was not.

## Mistranslation

What then shall we do with that text of St Paul? Shall we sadly dismiss it and say that Paul was being rather naïve? There is, of course, no reason why we should not feel free to do so. Every word of Scripture is not 'gospel'.

In fact, in this instance, it is possible to exonerate Paul, because he has been the victim of a mistranslation. The Western Church rendered his words in the version we have been considering:

> To them that love God, all things work together for good.

But the underlying Greek text can be translated as the Eastern Church has always rendered it:

> To them that love God, he [the Holy Spirit of the previous sentence], in all things, works together for good.

This throws a new light on the subject. We are talking now of the co-operation, not of things, but of God, and that is a completely different matter.

In this translation, we are no longer being asked naïvely to imagine the world as getting better and better, as if it were programmed for progress at all times. We know in our bones that this is not so, and that the world remains an ambiguous place, at times a downright hostile place. Things do not necessarily work together for our good.

But God does, even in the midst of a hostile world. When good things come our way in such a world, it is not because the world has been programmed to dispense them to us, but simply because they are a gift. Paul's hope is not based on a beneficent world, but on a good God. In context, his words read as follows:

> I reckon that the sufferings we now endure
> bear no comparison with the splendour, as yet unrevealed,
> which is in store for us.
> For the created universe waits with eager expectation
> for God's sons to be revealed.
> Creation was made the victim of frustration...
> and groans in all its parts
> as if in the pangs of childbirth...
> And even we, to whom the Spirit is given
> as firstfruits of the harvest to come,
> are groaning inwardly while we wait
> for God to make us his sons
> and set our whole body free...
> The same Spirit comes to the aid of our weakness.
> We do not even know how we ought to pray,

but through our inarticulate groans
the Spirit himself is pleading for us…
He pleads for God's people in God's own way;
and *in everything,* as we know,
*he co-operates for good with those who love God…*
With all this in mind, what are we to say?
If God is on our side, who is against us?…
Who will be the accuser of God's chosen ones?
It is God who pronounces acquittal; then who can condemn?…
What can separate us from the love of Christ?…
I am convinced that there is nothing in death or life,
in the realm of spirits or superhuman powers,
in the world as it is or the world as it shall be,
in the forces of the universe, in heights or depths –
nothing in all creation that can separate us
from the love of God in Christ Jesus our Lord.
(Romans 8:18-39, NEB)

Paul is describing the world as he sees it. It creaks and groans, it is frustrated and frustrating. It is a place of hardship and persecution, of calamity and finally death. And we are not to call these good, as if they are all working together for our wellbeing: they are clearly not. But we are to call them less strong than the love of God. The calamities remain calamities, not hidden blessings. But through all of them, God continues to work for our good.

Christians see the supreme example of this in the death of Jesus of Nazareth. Not that they point to the cross and say, 'Isn't that beautiful!' It was not: it was the epitome of evil. But if God can be present, as love, even in the midst of that, is there anywhere he is absent?

This too, of course, needs some believing. But it is a believing in God, not in things. It means trying to believe in a God who will not magically change things, who will let things be and not interfere to put them right, and whose presence therefore will often feel like an absence. It means trying to believe that in all things, in all circumstances, in all the events of our life, good and evil, we are loved; and that this love of God for us is stronger than all things put together.

False religion says, 'Do not fear. Trust in God, and he will see that none of the things you fear will happen'. True religion says, 'Do not fear. The things you fear may well happen to you, but they are nothing to be afraid of'.

No hardship, no kind of deprivation,
no persecution, suffering or pain,
in peace and war, no trouble, threat or danger,
nothing on the earth or in the heavens,
nothing that exists or is still to come,
nothing in our life, not even dying,
nothing can ever take away from us
the love of God that we have seen in Jesus;
nothing can ever separate us
from the love of God made real in Christ.
(Romans 8:35-39 tr. H. J. Richards)

O Lord, I am before your eyes
when I sit down and when I rise…
you guard me like a well fenced field,
your tender hand my sturdy shield…
If, like a bird, I climbed the air
or sank in hell, I'd find you there…
Before I crossed life's wilderness,
met with temptations or distress,
my path was traced with kindliness
by you, my God, whom now I bless.
O Lord, I am before your eyes
when I sit down and when I rise.
(Psalm 139 (138) tr. P. De Rosa)

God really *is* present, and more powerfully than we suspect, even when we feel abandoned. For nothing can ever separate us from his love.

## Questions for Discussion

• Is there a certain naïve improvidence about believing in Divine Providence?

• 'The knots at the back of the tapestry' is often proposed as a solution to the problem of evil. How acceptable do you find this?

• Should God be held responsible for natural disasters like floods, earthquakes, famine, drought, handicap, and so on?

# 6. On the Messiah:
## *what did Jesus claim?*

This chapter deals with the messianic hopes of the Old Testament. The word 'messianic' means 'relating to the Messiah'. The adjective is used here, rather than the noun, because the Old Testament hopes were far more varied than the word 'Messiah' might suggest. For the same reason, the plural word 'hopes' is used, rather than the singular.

### *The textbook approach*

There is a naïve view, strongly represented in some of the older textbooks, that the Old Testament expresses one single and consistent hope from the beginning to the end. All that the later books do is to fill in the finer detail omitted in the earlier ones, so that eventually people should know exactly what to look for.

The hope is first expressed in the opening pages of the book of Genesis, where Eve is promised that her seed will eventually crush the serpent. Later in the same book, the promise is repeated to Abraham, in whom all the nations of the world will find a blessing, and then narrowed down to the line of Isaac (not the Arabian Ishmael), the line of Jacob (not the Edomite Esau), and the Jewish line of Judah (not of the other Israelite tribes). The promise is fined down further in the person of David, who becomes the model for the hoped-for saviour and deliverer, and the hope is repeated by prophet after prophet as they look forward to a second David. The trump card is played by the last of the prophets, Daniel, who reveals that the saviour will actually come from heaven.

The other Old Testament books exist simply to provide more detail for these broad brush strokes. One text specifies that he will be born in Bethlehem, and another that a star will pinpoint the place. These are texts which foretell that he will be born of a virgin, that he will live in Nazareth, that he will journey to Egypt, and will return from there to visit the Temple. Other texts speak of his cleansing the Temple, of his entry into Jerusalem on an ass, and of his rejection by his own people. His death is precisely described – parched and pierced through, lying helpless between two creatures (or was that a reference to his birth between the ox and the ass?) His clothes will be diced for, he will be buried in a rich man's grave, his body will not corrupt in the tomb, and he will be raised up on the third day.

All these texts form a single and coherent picture. Anyone who does not see how accurately and exactly they are fulfilled in the life of Jesus of Nazareth is either a fool or a knave. Indeed, Jesus must have come close to despair as he wearily wondered how many more prophecies he must fulfil, ticking them off in his notebook one by one, before people recognised him as the one who had been foretold all along.

I have called this 'textbook' approach naïve because it gives the impression that the Old Testament had no other purpose than to foretell the future. It is as if God had nothing to say to people living at that time, only to the people of the New Testament. It is as if, when people yearned for an answer to the problems in their life, God said to them: 'I'm sorry I have nothing to tell you. But if you stay around for a few hundred years, you'll get a nice surprise.'

Obviously, the Old Testament is nothing like that. None of the texts referred to above is a direct foretelling of something in the distant future. All of them refer to something much more immediate, and the first readers recognised this. In other words, the texts were 'fulfilled' long before Jesus' time. To pick up these texts later on, and apply them to Jesus all over again as the New Testament does, is a very sophisticated use of the Old Testament. It involves a recognition of the far wider themes of which those texts are only occasional illustrations, and a profession of faith that in Jesus those wider themes find their fullness and completion.

The Old Testament messianic hopes are not to be reduced to a string of one-line prophecies. They are far more complex than that. They consist, rather, of a series of expectations born out of disillusionment. In other words, what the people of the Old Testament lived through was not a number of divine broadcasts telling them to be patient and wait. They lived, as all people have lived at all times, through a number of experiences which never came up to their expectations. The reality that they experienced always fell short of their hopes. What sort of experiences?

## Bible themes

1. Israel was born in the *Exodus* experience. About 1250 BC, a group of Israelite slaves escaped from Egypt under the leadership of Moses, and made their 'passover' into freedom. At the time, the experience must have felt like Kingdom Come. It was not long before they realised that it wasn't. Indeed, at some moments of their subsequent history, it must have seemed as if they had only exchanged one form of slavery for another. Clearly another (and deeper) Exodus-Passover would be needed (perhaps several), before God's plans could be said to have reached perfection. And this is precisely what the whole line of prophets preached, as they claimed to continue and complete the work of Moses. This, to the extent that the Qumran monks, and their disciple John the Baptist, set up their headquarters by the Jordan river, to indicate that the *Exodus-Passover-Moses* theme was still unfinished business. A new Moses was still to come.

2. The historical Exodus experience came to a conclusion about 1200 BC, in the setting up of an independent *Kingdom*. Not that the Israelites saw themselves as ruling the land of Palestine in their own right. They only held it in trust for God. But as the one land in the whole world where the kingship or rule of God was acknowledged and palpably experienced, it would hopefully attract all the surrounding nations to accept the rule of God, and so bring God's plans to completion. The hope was rudely shattered, over and over again. But it was never abandoned. Some day, the rule of God, so fitfully illustrated in the history of Israel, would become a world-wide reality, and the *Kingdom of God* established.

3. About 1000 BC, the Israelites elected to live under an *Anointed King*. This move was seen by many as a betrayal of the preceding theme, where kingship belonged to God alone. But for a while, a human king was acceptable on the condition that he acted only as God's stand-in or 'son', who did not rule from God's throne in the Temple, but from his palace to the south, at God's right hand. The arrangement, according to an enthusiastic tradition, worked perfectly under David, who brought his people unity, victory, peace and prosperity. But none of his successors, according to a pessimistic tradition, ever equalled his success, in spite of the prayers, as each was anointed (Hebrew *mashiah),* that God would raise another David. Indeed, who could live up to the hope that a king could deliver Israel from all that stood between her and God? Yet the hope survived, as prophets and psalms continued to reiterate the yearning for another *David, the anointed Mashiah-Christos, 'son' of God.*

4. The Jerusalem Temple was built about 950 BC to give tangible expression to the theme of *God's Presence* among his

people. This theme of a return to Paradise had already been outlined in the 'tabernacle' stories of Exodus times. But it finds its strongest expression after the monarchy had become defunct and hopes of a human 'son of God' began to be abandoned. Many of the psalms proclaim that the Lord (alone) is King, and the books written in the last few centuries BC express this hope in terms of *Divine Wisdom,* boldly personified, coming to dwell among God's people. (See Psalms 93-100, Isaiah 64, Ecclesiasticus 24.)

This short survey indicates that Old Testament messianism should not be spoken of simply in terms of *a* Messiah. The Messiah figures in only one out of four distinct themes. It was possible to express an authentic 'messianic hope' without looking forward to an individual Messiah. It is still manifestly possible to do so, as many Jews can bear witness. They should not be accused of being unfaithful to their Bible.

## *Christian titles*

This overview of the Jewish Bible enables us now to consider what the New Testament says about Jesus of Nazareth. It is clear, through the titles they give him, that its authors see him as the answer to all four unfulfilled hopes.

1. The *Exodus* theme is picked up in all the texts which see Jesus in terms of a new Moses. A concordance will reveal how strong this theme is in the New Testament. It is particularly strong in the Gospels of Matthew and John. Matthew deliberately divides his writing into five books, and entitles the first one (as the first of the five books of Moses is entitled in Greek) *Biblos Geneseos* or Book of Genesis (Matthew 1:1). John, too, begins his Gospel with the very same words which form the opening line (indeed, in Hebrew, the title) of the first book of Moses: 'In the beginning'. In these texts, and in many others,

Jesus is seen as the long-awaited second Moses, who completed the Exodus theme by bringing about the definitive Passover of the people of God into freedom.

2. The *Kingdom of God,* according to the synoptic Gospels, was the central theme of Jesus' own preaching. It is the subject of all the stories he told his audience, as he searched for image after image to express his vision. And it is the reason for the urgency of his message, for he saw the rule of God not in some utopian future, but a reality in becoming, here and now, in the midst of the people he was addressing. The Gospels maintain that in the life and death of Jesus, the Kingdom of God was a present reality.

3. The title of Messiah-Christ, or *Anointed King,* is one which is so readily applied to Jesus in the New Testament, especially by St Paul, that it almost becomes a surname. The title acknowledges him as the fulfilment of the yearning for another David, who brought about the peace which no Israelite king had ever been able to bestow on his people. The related title 'Son of God' is to be seen in this context. It is not in the first place a divine title, but a claim that he is the true King of Israel, the perfect human stand-in for God.

4. In contrast, the explicitly divine theme of *God's Presence* is heavily emphasised in the Gospel of John. There, Jesus is one who was with God from the beginning (indeed, 'was God'), and who became flesh in order to 'tabernacle' among us. To have seen him is to have seen the divine Glory, and to be in the very presence of God. Henceforth the true worship of God would be centred neither on Jerusalem nor on the Samaritan Gerizim, but on the divine Spirit flowing from his crucified body, for it is this which is to replace the soon-to-be-destroyed Temple. For Jesus is the answer to Isaiah's longing for Emmanuel –

God-with-us, and is appropriately given the title which pious Jews used in order to avoid the name of Yahweh – 'the Lord'.

Thus each of the four great Old Testament themes is taken up by the New Testament and applied to Jesus of Nazareth. Certainly its authors see him as the Messiah, but that is not saying the half of it. He is the answer to all the dreams in which the Old Testament had expressed its hopes of the future, and the moving force behind the whole of its history.

## How Jesus thought of himself

This is already saying a great deal about Jesus. But it does not yet tell us his own views on the subject. To what extent would he have approved of these claims? To what extent did he personally think of himself as 'the Christ'?

The question is a difficult one to answer. In the first place, we no longer have access to Jesus' own thoughts on the matter, only to the interpretations of the evangelists. That this is so, and cannot by the nature of things be otherwise, is so obvious that one would have thought it scarcely needed saying, were it not for the fact that most Christians continue to imagine that in the Gospel pages they are hearing the very words of Jesus first hand. They are not. They are hearing them at second hand, as Matthew, Mark, Luke and John have themselves interpreted what Jesus said of himself. This does not necessarily make those words less worthwhile. On the contrary. Wine is much more worthwhile than the grapes from which it is made. Nor can it be made without grapes. On the other hand, when I am offered wine, it is perverse to demand that it be reconstituted back into grapes.

The difficulty is compounded by the ambiguity of the only records we have about the matter. In some texts, Jesus seems to revel in the title: when the Samaritan woman in

John 4 yearns for the Messiah-Christ to come to solve her problems, Jesus is presented as declaring quite openly, 'I am he'. But on the other hand, there are texts in which he seems to be distinctly embarrassed by the title. In the story of Peter's profession of faith, where the speculations of the crowd are answered by Peter's bold, 'You are the Christ, the Son of God', Jesus is said (by all the evangelists) to forbid such words to be made public. Again, at the trial before Caiaphas, when Jesus is asked, 'Are you the Christ, the Son of God?', Matthew and Luke report him as replying, 'That is your title for me. The title I claim is "Son of Man".' Once more, at the trial before Pilate, when he is asked, 'Are you the King of the Jews?', all the evangelists represent him as replying, 'That is your word, not mine.' Luke even has Pilate agreeing that Jesus does not claim the title (Luke 23:4).

## Son of Man

All the evidence we have suggests that Jesus never laid claim to the title of Messiah-Christ at all. It is more than likely that he positively repudiated it, and that if he had been asked, 'Are you the Messiah?', he would have replied, 'Don't be silly'.

It would seem that the title he did use for himself was 'Son of Man'. The title occurs very frequently in the Gospels – up to eighty times – and is almost non-existent in the rest of the New Testament. It occurs in all four Gospels, and indeed in all of the most primitive strands of which the Gospels are made up. When it occurs, it is always used by Jesus about himself, never by others talking about him. All this suggests that 'Son of Man' was the most characteristic way in which Jesus spoke about himself.

But even if we can be reasonably certain that Jesus did claim this title for himself, there is absolutely no way in which we can be sure what he meant by it. In its most basic sense, it means no more than 'one who belongs to the category of man', in the same way that 'sons of Moab' simply means the Moabites, and 'sons of Israel' means the Israelites. A son of man is someone who belongs to the human race, a human being, Joe Soap, a polite circumlocution for 'I'.

The book of Ezekiel added some distinctive overtones to the title by using it nearly a hundred times to convey the weakness and fragility of Ezekiel himself, in contrast with the strength of God (the name Yehezek-el means 'God alone is the Strong One'). The book of Daniel gave the title quite a different slant by using it to convey the humanity of God's kingdom in contrast with the bestiality of the Babylonian, Persian and Greek kingdoms. These kingdoms, in vision after vision, are seen in terms of ravenous lions, bears and leopards. The kingdom of God, in contrast, is seen in terms of a 'Son of Man'. This is openly explained later in the text as a poetic summing up of the whole Israelite community, subsequently carried *up on the clouds* to be crowned by God himself (Daniel 7:13-27). This poetic image was so powerful that the latest writings of the Old Testament period turned it into an actual otherworldly person, pre-existent and scarcely distinguishable from God himself, who was expected to be carried *down on the clouds* to come and rescue Israel. This apocalyptic hope is expressed strongly in the apocryphal books of Enoch and 4 Esdras.

In which of these four senses (neutral, Ezekiel, Daniel, apocalyptic) is the title 'Son of Man' used in the Gospels? Strangely, at different times, in all four senses, though there is considerable emphasis on the apocalyptic figure of glory. But we have no means of knowing which sense would have been in the mind of Jesus. Could it be that, as he used it about himself, he intended the title to have only its weakest sense, meaning no more than 'I', a fellow human being, myself? Many scholars today would be inclined to say so, and to assume that the more pregnant overtones that the title now carries in the Gospels were read into it by the early Church. In which case, however strongly Jesus applied the title to himself, it gives us no clue whatever as to how he saw his role.

## Suffering Servant

If neither the title 'Christ' nor the title 'Son of Man' can give us any indication of who Jesus thought he was, where else can we turn? Perhaps to the title 'Suffering Servant', and to the many New Testament texts which speak of Jesus in this connection.

The latter half of the book of Isaiah seems to have been composed by a school of Isaiah's disciples, living in the Babylonian exile of the sixth century BC. There, having seen all the dire forebodings of their master painfully fulfilled, they turn to his more optimistic pages to yearn for the fulfilment of the more hopeful things he also said: 'Comfort ye, comfort ye, my people' (Isaiah 40:1).

Yet, strangely, their hopes are no longer pinned on the future royal descendant of David whom their master Isaiah had so longed for. Instead they introduce a most un-royal 'Servant of the Lord', apparently an embodiment of the Israel whom they see as the hope of the future. This ideal Israelite community is poetically described in four poems (chapters 42, 49, 50 and 53) as the obedient servant of God who will bring knowledge of the true God to a pagan world by its meek acceptance of suffering. The 'Servant' has himself learnt that suffering need not be a sign of God's rejection, but can on the contrary be a way of knowing God more intimately than ever before. Could the acceptance of 'death' at the hand of the world be the means of bringing knowledge of God to this world, and so of saving it?

Behold my Servant! He will triumph!…
As the world was once shocked at his fate –
disfigured beyond recognition…
so the world will now marvel,
its kings standing dumb in his presence…
'Who would believe [they say] what we have seen?…
For this Servant had no beauty to attract us…
a man of sorrows, familiar with grief…
Yet ours were the sufferings he bore…
We thought of his fate as punishment
inflicted upon him by God;
but he was wounded because of our sins,
he was crushed because of our guilt.
The punishment that fell on him has brought us peace;
the blows that fell on him have brought us healing…
The guilt that belonged to all of us
God has laid on his shoulders…
He never opened his mouth,
dumb as a lamb led to slaughter…
It never crossed anyone's mind
that he was being… done to death for our sins!…
It was God who willed he should be crushed,
so that when he had accepted his "death"
he would live a new life in his children,
and so accomplish the plan of God.'…
'Once his sufferings are over,' says God,
'he will again see the light and be rewarded,
and the world will win its acquittal
because my Servant has borne their guilt…
He has borne the guilt of the world,
the advocate of sinful men!'
(Isaiah 52:13-53:12, tr. H. J. Richards)

Jews have always understood this poem of theirs as an ide-
alisation of Israel. But it is applied to Jesus so frequently in
the New Testament (the margin of my Bible gives me 35
cross-references to places in the New Testament where this

passage is quoted) that it seems not impossible that Jesus modelled his ministry on these texts. He would be the ideal Israel who saved not only his own people, but the whole world, by revealing the true God even to those who killed him.

Many New Testament scholars are convinced that the title 'Suffering Servant' gives us a clearer insight into Jesus' mind than any other. But, of course, the image it evokes is far removed from the traditional image of the Messiah.

## *The Christ*

So we finally come to the crucial question, was Jesus the Messiah? In the strictest sense, no. It is probable that he never claimed the title for himself, and may even have expressly repudiated it. In any case, his life and work were in the event so strongly at odds with the image evoked by the Old Testament hope for a Messiah that one can hardly blame the Jews for saying that he is not the Christ. They, after all, had invented the idea, and they are entitled to say that Jesus does not fit it.

But then, even for Christians, there is a sense in which Jesus is not the Christ either. There is a strand of Christian belief, present from the earliest times onwards, which acknowledges that Jesus' life did not totally fulfil the hopes that the word 'Christ' contains. To complete what had been promised in the Old Testament, he would need to return with a power and a glory not shown in his first coming. And all those who profess their faith that 'he will come again in glory' share this belief.

If this is so, why on earth do Christians continue to call him 'the Christ'? He is given this title throughout the Gospel pages, particularly in John, and Paul uses it so freely that one could almost imagine it was Jesus' second name. Certainly for Christians today, the words 'Jesus' and 'Christ' are totally inter-changeable. Why have they done this? What do they mean?

They mean that Jesus is the model of what humanity is called to be. They mean that he reveals the destiny of the whole human race. They mean that he is the promise and guarantee of what human life can be like. They mean that he is the Christ, but only insofar as he anticipates the glory of the end days. He will be the Christ when all men and women have entered the glory which he has prefigured.

## Questions for Discussion

• Does this chapter's treatment of what used to be called 'Old Testament foretellings of Christ' make you feel cooler or warmer towards the Old Testament?

• If Jesus' life and work are so strongly at odds with the Jewish hope for a Messiah-Christ, how should Christians speak of him when they are in dialogue with Jews?

• The following New Testament texts make reference to the *Song of the Suffering Servant* in Isaiah 52:13-53:12. What do they tell us of the kind of Jesus the earliest Christians believed in?

Matthew 8:17; 26:28, 63, 67; 27:14, 29-31, 38, 58
Mark 15:28
Luke 22:37; 23:32
John 1:29; 12:24, 32, 38, 19:5, 18
Acts 3:13; 8:32-33
Romans 3:26; 4:25; 5:19; 10:16; 15:21
2 Corinthians 5:21
Galatians 3:13
Ephesians 1:20
Philippians 2:9
Colossians 2:15
Hebrews 2:10; 9:28
1 Peter 1:11; 2:22, 24-25; 3:18.

# 7. On Kingdom Come:
## *already or not yet?*

This chapter is a continuation of the last. We continue to search for what precisely it was that Jesus claimed to be, and what precisely the New Testament claims him to be, and what precisely Christians claim him to be.

Consider, for example, the Christian liturgical season of Advent. Although it is bracketed together with Lent as one of the two annual penitential seasons, it has none of the Lenten gloomy and guilt-ridden overtones. Looking forward to Christmas is something quite different from looking forward to Easter, and this is true not only for those who go to the shops, but also for those who go to church. There is something buoyant and uplifting in the Advent liturgy which the Lent liturgy never achieves. All our deepest hopes are addressed by a re-reading of the Old Testament which has not yet seen the Christ for whom it yearns. All our profound longings are aroused by the prayers and hymns with their make-believe that the Saviour of the world has not yet come:

O come, O come, Emmanuel,
O come, thou Rod of Jesse,
O come, thou Dayspring,
O come, thou Key of David,
O come, thou Lord of Might.

The Advent references to the Saviour are put into the future so that the subsequent feast of Christmas can once again be experienced as the answer to the world's prayer, and we are once again reassured that God's promised Kingdom has been successfully established on earth.

In these terms, the Christian conviction about Jesus is diametrically opposed to the Jewish one. A famous story has a Christian theologian trying to explain to a Jewish rabbi why he thinks the Messiah has come. The rabbi's reply is short and to the point. He simply looks out of the window and remarks, 'I see there's a cat and a dog fighting out there.' Clearly, as far as he is concerned, while we continue to exist in the kind of disharmony which allows cat to fight dog – or nation, nation, or Christian Jew – it is a little premature to talk about Kingdom Come.

## Past, present or future?

Eschatology, or the exploration of the ways in which God's plans for the world may be considered fulfilled, makes as good a starting point as any for discussing precisely what is at issue between Jews and Christians. In the simplest terms, the Jew sees the fulfilment of God's plans as a future event, the Christian as an event in the past and the present.

Christians are by definition people who believe in the Christ or Messiah as a demonstrable fact. For them the messianic days are not simply a hope for the future but a present reality. For them God's last word was spoken in the life of Jesus of Nazareth, and there is no other word (a different word, or an additional word) to wait for.

Non-Christians may be surprised to hear the Christian faith expressed in such absolute and final terms. In their daily living out of their lives, Christians do not seem to them to differ so much from the rest of the human race. Christians, like the rest of their brothers and sisters, seem to place their hopes and aspirations in the future rather than in the present. They give no indication that they regard the world they live in, beset as it is with danger, hardship and uncertainty, as a heaven on earth; it is a vale of tears, from which they hope eventually to escape into the eternal world to come. They may shout, 'We are saved' at the top of their voice, but they don't really behave as if they are, less still look like it.

All this is true. By and large, whatever their theoretical beliefs, Christians live in practice as if the messianic days are in the inaccessible future. They find nothing funny in the famous reply of the Jewish *stetl* elders, who refused to give their 'Watchman for the Messiah' the pay-rise he requested, 'because of the permanent nature of your employment'.

## Kingdom now?

In practice, then, the eschatology of Christians is as unrealised as it is for anyone else. They are surprised when scholars tell them that the many New Testament references to a future coming of the Christ are probably secondary, and that Jesus' original preaching seems to have been expressed in terms of the present, the here and now. His message was not, 'The Kingdom is coming soon', but, 'The Kingdom of God is in your midst'.

The finality of such words cannot be brushed aside. It is clear that Jesus regarded his word and work as bringing God's plans to crisis point. He spoke with a sense of urgency which demanded decision and commitment. Through his ministry the last times had come, and eternal choices had to be made. Scholars point out that in those parts of the New Testament which seem to echo his teaching most closely, the future-oriented hopes of his contemporaries are all transposed into the present: judgement is not in some distant future but now; the gift of the Holy Spirit is not tomorrow but today; eternal life and the kingdom of 'the heavens' is a reality to be lived not in an afterlife but in the present. The finality of Jesus' preaching has to be taken seriously, not least by those who claim to live by his teaching.

And yet this too needs to be qualified. It is equally clear

that, however urgently he spoke, Jesus was reluctant – to say the least – to assume the title of Messiah when it was offered him. Those who wish to acknowledge him as the Christ have to beware of attributing to him pretensions he clearly never had. He never for a moment claimed that in his ministry the age-old expectations of his people were fulfilled. Indeed any child could see that they were not, if cats still fought with dogs, and lambs refused to lie down with lions.

In what sense, then, was the message of Jesus so final? Why, in that case, did he lay such emphasis on the present moment? What was so new about his teaching that demanded such urgent commitment?

Nothing, surely, except the reapplication of a timeless insight into the ways of God with the world. He did not claim to preach a strange new doctrine. He was only saying in a new way what had always been God's message to his people: that he is a God who summons them out of death, and again and again opens for them the door to life.

## Ultimates now

The ultimate choices are therefore always urgently before us, and we experience the mystery of life and death in each 'now'. That is to say, the problems of the world we live in cannot be shrugged off into another world – indeed the prophets knew nothing of such a world. It is in our world, the only world we know, that the Kingdom has to be made into a reality, and the only time for doing that is now. Salvation is constantly near, because it is constantly in the hands of people to make it or mar it. The question people must ask themselves is not when the creation of a new world will be brought about, but how? Their eyes must be focused not on the horizon, but on their own heart.

What the whole of Judaism had been about, from the very beginning, was the utter seriousness of the life that people live in God's world. As a true Jew, Jesus preached nothing different. As a successor of the prophets, he wanted to do nothing other than see the world of people with the eyes of God. Hence the urgency, and in a sense the finality, of his message.

But it should be clear by now that the finality is no different from the finality preached by the prophets. On this score, there is no reason whatever why those who glory in the teaching of the prophets should find themselves at daggers drawn with those who glory in the teaching of Jesus.

Of course Jews must continue to proclaim an unrealised eschatology, but not to the extent that they obscure the fact that it can only be realised in the present moment. And of course Christians must continue to emphasise that present moment, but not to the extent that they begin to identify their Church with Kingdom Come, which it manifestly is not. The eschatological hope lies in a fine tension between present and future, between the realised and the unrealised, between the 'already' and the 'not yet'. Neither Jews nor Christians can afford to release that tension if they wish to remain in dialogue.

## Dividing lines

When basic tenets are radically examined, even in faiths as deeply divided as Christianity and Judaism, the dividing lines are discovered not to be where they have traditionally been put. In fact they may be discovered not to exist at all. Jews do well to pin their hopes on the future, but when they reflect on the secular and historical nature of their faith, their eschatology may be more realised than they realise. Similarly Christians do well to proclaim that salvation is today and not tomorrow, but they too will admit, when pressed, that in reality this is less present than the Christian case sometimes presents.

For, when all is said and done, if the claims that Christians make were as exclusive as is sometimes imagined, then the only attitude they could take towards those of other faiths would be one of domination, and any talk of dialogue would simply be a piece of pious humbug. Christians who are really serious about dialogue with non-Christians must be prepared to answer some searching questions about their own faith, first among which would be: 'In what sense do you claim that Jesus *is* the Christ?'

If the New Testament claims for Jesus are as absolute and final as they sound, do they leave any real breathing space for other religions? Is the fear of other religions, and the desire to dominate them, only incidental to Christianity, a regrettable human failing, or is it built into the very Gospels on which Christianity is founded? In particular, is the anti-Judaism implicit in Christianity so integral to the Christian message that its removal will make the message itself disintegrate?

If Jesus is the one mediator between God and the world, outside of whom there is no salvation, can a disciple of his do anything other than wish to turn all people into Christians, especially the Jews who explicitly refuse him that title? In other words, can a Christian say, 'Jesus is Messiah' without adding under his breath, 'and Jews be damned'?

If Christianity is the 'fulfilment' of everything the prophets promised, how can Christians tolerate a reading of the prophets which does not acknowledge this? If the Church is the New Israel, indeed the True Israel, how can Judaism continue to have the right to exist?

Is the answer that Christians must be willing to see God's grace operative everywhere, not only in the Church? But does that mean that all non-Christians are simply 'implicit Christians'? Are they eventually destined simply to be swallowed up by the explicit Christianity of the Church? Have other religions no validity in their own right? How would

Christians react to being called 'implicit Buddhists'?

Is the trouble that Christian claims for Jesus have been too absolute, even in the New Testament? Do Christians perhaps need to re-think their Christology, to qualify the titles they have given to Jesus? To admit that he is not yet 'The Christ' in the full sense of that word, that in a most profound sense the Kingdom of God has not yet arrived, and that the Christian, no less than any other believer, must work for its coming?

The Christian will find these disturbing questions. The fact that they are beginning to be asked is for some a sign of the disintegration of Christianity. For others it is a harbinger of the real dialogue that can now at long last replace the charades that we have so far been playing.

## Questions for Discussion

- If Christians still turn to the future to await the establishment of God's Kingdom ('Thy Kingdom come'), how precisely do they differ from Jews?

- If the New Testament claims for Jesus are as absolute and final as they sound, do they leave any real breathing space for other religions?

- When today's Christian theologians are reluctant to be as absolute about Jesus as the New Testament is, are they breathing new life into Christianity, or killing it off?

# 8. On the Jews:
## *is the New Testament anti-Jewish?*

When Theodore Hertzl was asking in 1904 for recognition of his projected Jewish State, the 'saintly' Pope Pius X replied, on behalf of the Roman Catholic Church: 'The Jews did not recognise our Lord; we cannot recognise the Jewish people.'

The dedication of David Kossoff's *The Book of Witnesses* (Fount, 1978) is expressed in the following words: 'This book is for my father, who died long ago. Once, when I was small, about eight, I was with my father, who was a loving man, in a narrow street in the East End. A huge labourer suddenly roared down at us that we had killed Jesus. My father asked him why he was so unhappy, and the fist lowered and the shouting stopped and he began to cry. We took him with us to my aunt for tea. This book is for my father, who was a loving man.'

A letter appeared in the Catholic press a little while ago, written in alternating black and red ink. It ran as follows:

Nature and the universe are not as simple as Einstein and his Godless friends and backers wanted us to believe. Let this be a lesson and a warning to all the evil and sinister and demonic scientist socialist Jews and to all their gentile hirelings and followers who still believe that they can destroy and replace God's universe and Holy Bible with their theories ... These Godless scientific socialist Jews are always boasting that their theories are ruling the world, but there is news for these Jews, and the news is that their theories will not be ruling the world for much longer. The wrath of God is coming down on these evil and sinister scientific-socialist

Jews and on their evil and demonic and crazy theories that rule the world!!! PS. The Jews are not really Jews any more, but they are Protestants. The Christians are the real Jews now.

## Alive and well

The quotations may serve to reassure anyone who needs reassuring, that anti-Semitism is alive and well, even among Christians. The cognoscenti would say, 'Especially among Christians'. They would not expect sentiments of that kind from Muslims, or humanists, or atheists. Is there something built into Christianity which inevitably makes it anti-Semitic? Is anti-Semitism such an integral part of the Christian message that it cannot be eliminated without destroying the Gospel?

The suggestion may shock some Christians. Surely, they would say, the occasional anti-Jewish passage in the New Testament is peripheral, and has nothing to do with its central message. Surely, they would say, the tirades of the early Church Fathers against the Jews were due to a misinterpretation of the Gospel, not to the Gospel itself. Surely, they would say, the long history of anti-Semitism in Europe has a secular explanation, and has really nothing to do with religion, only with a disastrous misunderstanding of religion.

There are many good people, including Christians, who think otherwise. They would agree with the Jew who said: 'Anyone who wants to know all about the Christians should read the Sermon on the Mount. Anyone who wants to know more about the Christians should read the history of their relationship with the Jews.' The fact is that the anti-Semitism which has been characteristic of the history of Christian Europe would simply have been impossible if it had not been deeply thought to be an essential part of the Gospel message. The systematic persecution of Jewish communities, which resulted in their total exclusion from England by the year

1300, and from the whole of western Europe by the year 1500, and which finally allowed Nazism (with hardly a voice raised in protest) to perpetrate a Holocaust in which one third of world Jewry was exterminated – all this simply could not have happened without the backing of the Gospel. Hitler boasted to two protesting bishops that he was only practising what they had been preaching for 2000 years. No country under Islamic rule ever acted like this. The anti-Jewish impetus seems to be rooted in the Gospel itself. It is experienced as part of the Gospel message, even by people who cannot bring themselves to admit it.

## *The Gospel as absolute*

Fifty years ago, no Christian could have thought that, let alone said it. With the views we had then of inspiration and inerrancy, such a suggestion was impossible. The Gospel was gospel. Whatever it said, or even implied, was divine, eternal and absolute. Nor did it matter whether it was said by Jesus, or by Matthew quoting Jesus, or only by Matthew himself: all of it was gospel.

It is only within the last fifty years that our understanding of the Gospel has become less rigid and less absolute. Jesus is now allowed to be Jesus, and not an abstract person from another world. And Matthew is allowed to be Matthew, and not just undifferentiated 'gospel'. He is even allowed to be ignorant, or prejudiced, or just plain wrong; he is after all human.

Our previous understanding of the Gospel was much stricter. If Jesus spoke of his patients as 'demoniacs', and treated them as such, then demoniacs is what they were: he had divinely revealed it. If Matthew's Jesus spoke in blistering terms of the Pharisees, then Jesus had condemned Pharisaic Judaism for all time. After all, we said when we were challenged, some of the Pharisees of Jesus' time were highly objectionable, as they even admitted themselves, and that justifies the harsh language of the Gospel. And after all, Jesus and Matthew were themselves Jews, and therefore entitled to be brutally frank with their brother Jews. But these passages of the Gospel (it was claimed) could not possibly be taken as a piece of anti-Semitism. Since they are part of the Gospel, they could not possibly be prejudiced. That would be a contradiction in terms. Those who made these passages into a platform for anti-Semitism were simply insensitive Christians, who read their own prejudices into an otherwise innocent text.

## *The Gospel as relative*

Today we are no longer so rigid in our understanding of the Gospel. We no longer find it necessary to make every sentence consistent with every other sentence. We know that the sentences were not dictated from heaven. They were the expression of the minds of a dozen different authors, and these are allowed to have viewpoints as different as any other dozen. Nor do we find it necessary to treat every quotation mark as a guarantee that we are listening to the actual words spoken by Jesus. The evangelist does not claim to give us anything other than his personal interpretation of Jesus' teaching, and this interpretation is inevitably going to reflect the background against which he writes his Gospel, which may be anything from thirty to seventy years distant from Jesus himself. This must clearly be allowed for, else we will make Jesus say things he could not possibly have said, being outside his range.

So for example, when Jesus said, 'My followers must take up the cross', he presumably meant that they must be willing to face such opposition as might eventually lead them to the gallows. When Luke changes that saying into a command to take up the cross 'daily', he has made it, in more peaceful times, into a rule of Christian life, where 'crosses' must be borne day by day - and so considerably weakened the original stark saying.

Or again, the explanation of the parable of the Sower offered in the Gospel of Mark, and faithfully copied by Matthew and Luke, refers pessimistically to the dangers of lapsing from Christianity for materialistic ends. This 'explanation' is clearly influenced by the circumstances of the Christian communities growing up in the 70s and 80s of the first century. It would have had no meaning whatever for the original Galilean audience in the 30s to whom Jesus tells what is in fact a rather optimistic story of an abundant harvest in spite of all the incidental losses.

Again, there are numerous passages in the Gospel which make it clear that the title 'Messiah-Christ' was one which Jesus accepted with great reluctance, if indeed he ever accepted it at all. How is it, then, that the Jesus of John's Gospel is presented as declaring quite openly, 'I am the expected Messiah' (John 4:26)? Because by the time John was writing, that is the title that all Christians had given to Jesus.

## Jesus the Jew

To return to the question of anti-Semitism and anti-Jewish prejudice. Many pages of the Gospel speak of a relationship between main-line Judaism and the followers of Jesus which is true to the 70s and 80s when the Gospels were written, but is not true to the 30s when Jesus was preaching. The simplest example is the word 'Jew', which the Gospel of John uses regularly as a synonym for 'The Opposition'. This has influenced his readers so deeply that there are some Christians who are unaware that Jesus was himself a Jew, and those who are aware find it something of an embarrassment. John's language and attitude would have been quite impossible in

99

Jesus' lifetime, where a Jewish Jesus, surrounded by exclusively Jewish disciples, was addressing a totally Jewish audience. No distinction could have been made at that time between being a Jew and being a follower of Jesus. That distinction, now developed and hardened, belongs to the time when the Gospel was written. In short, Jesus was not anti-Jewish. John was.

Similar critical observations must be made about the word 'Pharisee' – the Pharisees whom the Gospels represent as the leaders of the opposition to Jesus, indeed the agents of his death. This hardly squares with the fact that much of Jesus' teaching is echoed in the teaching of great rabbis of his time, and that a number of prominent Pharisees became disciples of Jesus – Nicodemus, Joseph of Arimathea, Saul of Tarsus. It squares least of all with the fact that far from wielding power in the time of Jesus, the Pharisees were only a minority opposition group. The powers-that-be were the high priestly families and the Sadducees – and it is these whom the Acts of the Apostles correctly represent as persecuting the infant church as they had persecuted Jesus.

The Pharisees only assumed leadership after the year 70, when the Temple had been destroyed and the priesthood made redundant. The situation which then obtained, of an official rabbinical Judaism at loggerheads with the followers of Jesus, has been read back into the Gospels, as if it had obtained in the lifetime of Jesus. But it did not. Jesus is represented as saying, 'They will drive you out of the synagogues' (John 9:22, 16:2), although this kind of excommunication did not become Jewish practice until the year 90, that is to say 60 years after Jesus. Similarly, Jesus is represented as saying, 'It is written in your Law' (John 8:17, 10:34, 15:25). Jesus could not have used such words. For him it was 'our Law'.

It is clear, then, that the circumstances in which the

Gospels were written have deeply influenced their approach, and have modified even the way in which Jesus is represented as speaking. The Jesus of Matthew's Gospel launches the most vehement attack on Judaism, in a well-known passage:

> Woe to you, scribes and Pharisees, hypocrites!
> because you shut the kingdom of heaven against men;
> for you neither enter yourselves,
> nor allow those who would enter to go in.
>
> Woe to you, scribes and Pharisees, hypocrites!
> for you traverse sea and land to make a single proselyte,
> and when he becomes a proselyte,
> you make him twice as much a child of hell as yourselves ...
>
> Woe to you, scribes and Pharisees, hypocrites!
> for you tithe mint and dill and cummin,
> and have neglected the weightier matters of the law,
> justice and mercy and faith ...
>
> Woe to you, scribes and Pharisees, hypocrites!
> for you cleanse the outside of the cup and of the plate,
> but inside they are full of extortion and rapacity ...
>
> Woe to you, scribes and Pharisees, hypocrites!
> for you are like whitewashed tombs,
> which outwardly appear beautiful,
> but within they are full of dead men's bones and
>     all uncleanness ...
>
> Woe to you, scribes and Pharisees, hypocrites!
> for you build the tombs of the prophets and adorn [them] ...
> [and] witness against yourselves
> that you are sons of those who murdered the prophets.
>
> Fill up, then, the measure of your fathers.
> You serpents, you brood of vipers,
> how are you to escape being sentenced to hell?
> (Matthew 23:13-33)

As an analysis of the potential hypocrisy which lies at the heart of any religion, including Christianity, this page of the New Testament will always retain its value. But it wasn't Jesus who felt like this about the Judaism of his time. It was Matthew, about the Judaism of his later time. Even so, the page eventually became 'gospel', and so dictated the attitude which Christians would take towards Jews ever since. These Christians did not misinterpret the Gospel. They got it absolutely right, exactly as Matthew had intended. The animosity which has marked their relationship with Jews is not some terrible mistake; it is rooted in the pages of the Gospel. And as long as the Gospel is read in an absolutist way, as the direct Word of God, dictated by heaven, that animosity will continue.

## Paul

When we turn from the Gospel of Matthew to the earlier Gospel of Paul, the situation becomes even more complicated. Here, Christianity and Judaism had not yet become two opposing camps. Paul wrote his letters before that had taken place. Paul's situation is more personal, and has to do with his own ambiguous feelings about his conversion. He had been a fanatical anti-Christian. He had become an ardent supporter of Christianity.

He copes with this personal problem by polarisation. In other words, he applies all his good feelings to Christianity, and offloads all his bad feelings on to Judaism. As he reads his Old Testament, written by Jews for Jews, he divides all its statements into positive ones and negative ones. He interprets all the positive ones as promises made to the Christians – salvation, glory and union with God. All the negative ones he applies to the Jews – blame, guilt, odium, reproach and condemnation.

In Romans 9-11, Israel is described as blind, deaf, dead, carnal and stupid. The Torah of the Jews is abrogated and they have lost the right to exist. The promises once made to them have all been fulfilled in Christianity, and their one-time election as God's People is now only a burden, an albatross round their neck. Paul agrees with John's Gospel that Judaism has been a failure, not only when it confronted Jesus, but through its whole history. Jews have always preferred the flesh to the spirit, the false to the true, self-righteousness to trust in God. They are the embodiment of all that is unredeemed, perverse, stubborn, evil and demonic.

It is true that, in the midst of this diatribe, Paul's intense fellow feelings for the Jews keep breaking through. He says he would even accept his own damnation if that could benefit them. He yearns for their salvation even more than for his own. Yet none of this can disguise or neutralise the vehemence with which he condemns them. Is it any wonder that people like St John Chrysostom were able to develop Paul's chapters into a whole literature entitled *Against the Jews?* 'God has always hated the Jews', he says, 'and so do I.' He didn't sadly misunderstand Paul. He understood him very well indeed.

Perhaps we should understand Paul too, against his background and the difficulties with which he had to contend. And in the light of the magnificent insights he has elsewhere given us, perhaps we can even forgive him. What we must not do is to absolutise him, either in his insights, or (less still) in his blind spots. But we must recognise that those blind spots remain part of the New Testament.

In other words, even the New Testament, Word of God though we Christians acknowledge it to be, must not be made into an absolute. The Word of God has to be heard in every event of the history of our world, not least in Christendom's abortive attempt finally to rid the world of Judaism. The Word which God speaks in events of this kind may demand that we re-examine what we previously took too finally to be the Word of God.

## Questions for Discussion

- Is it possible to reconcile the blatant prejudice in some passages of the Bible with the doctrine of scriptural inerrancy as commonly understood?

- Paul the Jew wrote some painfully strong words about his fellow Jews (see especially Philippians 3; Romans 9-11; Galatians 3:13; 4:9 and 5:12). To what extent are non-Jews entitled to make his words their own?

- The 'conversion of the Jews' is one of the New Testament's deepest concerns. Today many Christians are happy simply to 'dialogue' with Jews. Are they being unfaithful to the New Testament?

# 9. On the Chosen People:
## *chosen for what?*

A greetings card that recently came my way has a line draw-ing of Jonah and the whale on the front, with the text: 'The Lord prepared a great fish to swallow up Jonah. Then Jonah prayed unto the Lord his God out of the fish's belly.' The greeting inside reads: 'And the Lord spake unto the fish, and it vomited out Jonah upon the dry ground. Good wishes.' One has seen greetings expressed more elegantly.

### *The joke*

Or was it that the publishers were simply capitalising on the fact that the book of Jonah is one enormous joke? A joke? Was there not an actual prophet called Jonah? Yes indeed; 2 Kings 14:25 refers to a prophet of that name operating in Israel about the year 750 BC, when Assyria ruled the Middle East from its capital Nineveh. Yet that text breathes not a word about any miraculous Mediterranean cruise, let alone about the phenomenal conversion of the Assyrian Empire. Isn't this odd? Might one not have expected at least an allu-sion to these marvels?

What is odder still is that the book of Jonah, though it is included in the collection of all other prophetical books, is quite unlike all the others. The others all present the preach-ing of the prophet, with only an occasional piece of narrative to put that preaching in its context. The book of Jonah is all narrative, and contains only eight words of actual preaching: 'Yet forty days, and Nineveh shall be overthrown!' Are we not right to smell something fishy?

The book is further enlivened by a series of remarkable miracles, the like of which not even the 'major' prophets could boast. They seem to occur at the drop of a hat. A whole pagan nation is converted by a single sentence, a miracle far outstripping Pentecost. Jonah is halted in his tracks by a miraculous storm. The sailors are miraculously converted to the true God. The sea miraculously calms once Jonah is overboard. A miraculous psalm issues from the whale's mouth. Jonah is provided shade by a miraculous plant. The plant is killed off by a miraculous worm. People who find the whale hard to swallow ought to be made aware that the whale is the least of the book's problems.

An even greater problem has been posed by the literary critics. Literary criticism is able to establish, fairly confidently, the origin of a piece of writing by examining closely its vocabulary, style, interests, allusions and use of quotations. When the book of Jonah is subjected to this kind of criticism, it is clear that it was written long after the Babylonian exile, about 450 BC. Why should an author of that time recount the Mediterranean adventures of a prophet living three hundred years earlier, long before the exile? Does the clue to the meaning of the book lie here?

To reconstruct the life of post-exile Israel – its ideas, thoughts, priorities, hopes and fears – might reveal a great deal about the purpose of this book. Anyone neglecting to do so might miss the whole point of it. It would be like reading *Gulliver's Travels* under the impression that it was a timeless travelogue. This is the way children read it, and not without profit, since it is a brilliant work of imagination. But they remain totally ignorant of Swift's satirical purpose. The only reason he wrote the book was to poke fun at the politics of the eighteenth century, and it goes right over their heads.

Are we like children when we read the book of Jonah without putting it into its context? Are we missing the whole point of the book? Poor author! Was he being too clever for us?

## *The context*

The post-exile period of Israel's history, 500-400 BC, was one of the most crucial that the nation had to live through. In its way, it was as critical as the exile itself, where Israel had to learn to accept a kind of death if it was going to have any future.

Israel survived the exile. The return from Babylon was like a resurrection:

> When the Lord delivered Zion from bondage
> it seemed like a dream;
> then was our mouth filled with laughter,
> on our lips there were songs …
> Those who sow in tears and sorrow
> will reap one day with joy.
> (Psalm [125] 126, Grail)

And the harvest was indeed substantial. A renewed Israel, transformed by suffering, took the road back to its ancestral land filled with the highest ideals. The ruined capital of Jerusalem was rebuilt with energy and zeal, and a new temple dedicated like the crown for a queen. What more could Israel do? Now it was up to God. Was this Kingdom Come?

The discovery that it wasn't, that life was going to go on as uniform and drab and fraught as ever – this was an anti-climax that few could cope with. Many lost their faith altogether. The others resigned themselves to a kind of weary formalism and a purely mechanical fulfilment of their religious duties. It was as if God would have to be satisfied with that if he did not come up with his part of the bargain.

Many of the Old Testament books written at this time give evidence of a religion practised without joy. Malachi complains of insincere liturgy. The priestly compendium now called Ezra-Nehemiah-Chronicles is an indictment of Israel's religion and calls for urgent reform. The latest additions to the book of Isaiah carry the sort of sharp criticism which inspired Robert Herrick to offer the following translation of Isaiah 58:6-10:

> Is this a fast, to keep
>   the larder lean? And clean
> from fat of veales and sheep?
>
> Is it to quit the dish
>   of flesh, yet still to fill
> the platter high with fish?
>
> Is it to fast an hour,
>   or ragg'd go, or show
> a downcast look, and sour?
>
> No: 'tis a fast, to dole
>   thy sheaf of wheat and meat
> unto the hungry soul.
>
> It is to fast from strife,
>   from old debate and hate;
> to circumcise thy life.
>
> To show a heart grief-rent,
>   to starve thy sin, not bin;
> and that's to keep thy Lent.

But there are worse things than perfunctory religion. There is a religion that is narrow-minded and bigoted, intolerant and inward-looking. The exile, far from widening Israel's outlook, had made it more exclusively nationalistic than ever before. In post-exile Israel, the hatches were down and the shutters closed with a vengeance.

This characteristic of Israelite religion is also reflected in the writings of this time. The prophet Malachi is totally opposed to mixed marriages. His colleague Joel revels in the prospect of the nations receiving God's come-uppance in the valley of Jehoshaphat as they attack a beleaguered Jerusalem.

Ezra's ambition is to make the Torah into a 'hedge' that will isolate his people. Nehemiah turns that dream into bricks and mortar as he sets about building a wall around Jerusalem. The Chronicler re-writes the whole of past history to represent Israel eternally as a race apart. It is a setting where Hilaire Belloc, with his 'Noel, Noel, may all Protestants go to hell', would have felt deeply at home.

## Jonah the anti-hero

When the book of Jonah is placed into this setting, it suddenly speaks with a new voice. Who is this self-righteous fanatic howling for the destruction of the pagans? Why, it is the fifth century BC People of God! And what does God think about it? He doesn't like it at all!

Slowly the joke begins to register. Slowly we begin to notice that this apparently innocent little book has a wicked grin. Slowly it dawns on us that Jonah is not the hero of the story at all. In fact he is a kind of anti-hero, the very antithesis of the classical prophet.

When the Word of the Lord comes to Jonah, he doesn't fall on his knees like Isaiah or Jeremiah saying, 'Lord, I am not worthy'. On the contrary, he thumbs his nose at God. In fact, having been told to go east and preach God's word in the Assyrian capital of Nineveh, he rushes down to Tel Aviv to catch the first boat west as far as he can go, to Gibraltar.

Can one blame him? When Assyria had ruled the Middle East three hundred years earlier, it was not only the most powerful empire the world had ever known, but also the most barbarous. The walls of its palaces were covered with friezes depicting scenes of the utmost cruelty. The frenzied passion with which the prophet Nahum looks forward to the fall of Nineveh bears eloquent witness to the loathing which Assyria was able to inspire across the whole Mediterranean world:

Disaster to the city of blood,
packed throughout with lies,
stuffed with booty,
where plundering has no end! ...
The cunning witch
who enslaved nations by her harlotries
and tribes by her spells ...
Who has not felt
your unrelenting cruelty?
(Nahum 3:1-19, NJB)

It has been suggested that God's command that Jonah preach in Nineveh was rather like the Chief Rabbi in 1941 being told to convert Hitler, Goering and Goebbels in Berchtesgaden. But even Nazism cannot be compared to Nineveh for the sheer horror it evoked – more bestial than Belsen, and more gruesome than the Gulags.

## God's strange purpose

Yet the conversion of Nineveh, says the author of this little book, is part of the strange purpose of God. Its inhabitants have as much right to be called the People of God as Israel. So that when Jonah runs as far as he can from that divine purpose, God has to resort to every device in his repertoire – the raging storm, the man overboard, the great whale – to bring him back to square one. 'As I was saying before we were so rudely interrupted – to Nineveh, please!' The strange purpose will not be thwarted.

The storm and the whale are probably intended as symbols of the Babylonian exile from which Israel had recently returned. This would make Jonah's psalm, sung from the depths of the whale, highly appropriate: it looks forward to the return to Jerusalem. At the time, the prophet Jeremiah had spoken of the exile as a great monster which threatened to make mincemeat of Israel (Jeremiah 51:34, 44). On the contrary, our author seems to be saying, the exile was God's device to force Israel to understand its mission, which is to bring knowledge of the true God to the whole pagan world.

So Jonah is given his marching orders a second time: to Nineveh. And this time he does not go by whale-way. The result of the journey is remarkable. After eight words, Nineveh is on its knees. Quite an achievement when one remembers the scant success of the preaching of the classical prophets. An almost unbelievable achievement when one is aware of Nineveh's reputation for brutality and beastliness.

But far from being overwhelmed by his success, Jonah is furious. This is a death-bed conversion! It's not fair!

> It displeased Jonah exceedingly, and he was angry. And he prayed to the Lord and said, 'I pray thee, Lord, is not this what I said when I was yet in my country? That is why I made haste to flee to Tarshish [Gibraltar]; for I knew that thou art a gracious God and merciful, slow to anger, and abounding in steadfast love, and repentest of evil. Therefore now, O Lord, take my life from me, I beseech thee, for it is better for me to die than to live.'
>
> And the Lord said, 'Do you do well to be angry?' Then Jonah went out of the city and sat to the east of the city, and made a booth for himself there. He sat under it in the shade, till he should see what would become of the city.
>
> And the Lord God appointed a plant, and made it come up over Jonah, that it might be a shade over his head, to save him from his discomfort. So Jonah was exceedingly glad because of the plant. But when dawn came up the next day, God appointed a worm which attacked the plant, so that it withered. When the sun rose, God appointed a sultry east wind, and the sun beat upon the head of Jonah so that he was faint; and he asked that he might die, and said, 'It is better for me to die than to live.' But God said to Jonah, 'Do you do well to be angry for the plant?' And he said, 'I do well to be angry, angry enough to die' (Jonah 4:1-9).

The petulance is that of a child. Let the great city be annihilated to vindicate the chosen race, but give Jonah back his little umbrella!

## An apologetic God

The closing words of this short story provide the punch line:

> And the Lord said, 'You pity the plant, for which you did not labour, nor did you make it grow, which came into being in a night, and perished in a night. And should not I pity Nineveh, that great city, in which there are more than a hundred and twenty thousand persons who do not know their right hand from their left, and also much cattle?' (Jonah 4:10-11)

Man shouting for vengeance, and God having to apologise for being more merciful – what a brilliant ending.

The fact is, of course, that exclusivism leads to the ultimate in blasphemy. The logic of his position forces the exclusivist, in the name of religion, to set himself above God.

'Lord, you want to offer salvation to non-Catholics? Don't be absurd! People will think you're suggesting that salvation is available for non-Christians too, these Jews and Muslims. How ridiculous! You'll be saying next that you can even find a place for non-believers, for atheists and humanists! You must be off your head! You don't know what you're doing. You'll ruin the name of religion!'

'O, I'm so sorry, Jonah. Please forgive me. I do apologise.'

Jonah is an accurate portrait of the Israel of the fifth century BC. Jonah with his obstinacy and petulance, with his selfishness and narrowness, with his crying need to repudiate others in order to vindicate himself – is an accurate portrait of the People of God of any century, BC or AD. We praise God for his mercy towards us, but deplore such mercy being shown to others, who clearly do not deserve it as we do. We bewail the loss of our little umbrellas – the securities we depend on, the cushions we have provided against discomfort in this world and the next – but long for the destruction of Nineveh. And God can only apologise 'I'm afraid your ideas about me are rather narrow. I'm actually rather larger than that.'

The message that Jonah preached, of course, did not differ from the message of all the other prophets. 'Yet forty days, and Nineveh shall be overthrown' is precisely what Isaiah had said about Edom, and Jeremiah about Babylon, and Nahum (in as many words) to Nineveh itself. But what right has anyone to take these words as absolute rather than conditional? Surely even the threatening words of God are an expression of his mercy, addressed to people who would not otherwise take note of what he is saying. Surely when sinners do take note, they are as dear to God as those who smugly hug their Linus blankets. Perhaps even more dear and near to God, since their love is more genuine.

The book of Jonah is a kind of manifesto of God's mercy and forgiveness. When the New Testament finally says explicitly, 'God is love', we are not to imagine that this good news has never been proclaimed before. Each of this book's short chapters has ended with a picture of God showing mercy: to the sailors in danger of shipwreck, to Jonah in danger of being digested, to Nineveh in danger of not finding God, and finally to Jonah himself in danger of not really knowing that God at all.

## Jonah the 'schlemiel'

Perhaps it is worth asking, finally, about Jonah himself: how in the last analysis do we judge him? As a felon or as a fool? A criminal or a cretin? A monster or a moron?

On the one hand, he is the only unlovable person in the whole story. All the other characters endear themselves immediately – the pagan sailors, the king of Nineveh, the citizens, even the much cattle. The only villain of the piece is Jonah, the great prophet of the Lord.

On the other hand, his very lack of grace melts the heart. Throughout the story he is the classical fall-guy, the born loser, the half-wit who is so immersed in himself that he doesn't know what's going on. An almighty storm is raging upstairs, and he's below deck asleep. He converts the pagan sailors to the true God without even trying. He is swallowed by a whale, and all he can think of is to settle in as comfortably as he can. His preaching converts the whole of Nineveh when he was trying to do the very opposite. In the first chapter he is floored by a whale, and in the last by a worm. What better example of a Yiddish *schlemiel,* the imbecile who keeps coming a cropper? He is the one who, in the last analysis, is most in need of God's pity. And he gets it, even though he begrudges it to others.

How we judge Jonah may tell us something about the way we judge ourselves. Am I the sinner whom even God can't forgive? Or am I just the poor simpleton who can't hear God even when he's shouting at me, to whom God has to say, 'Never mind. I'll call again. Please forgive me.'

People ask whether the book of Jonah is true. Can anything be more true than the message contained in these few lines?

## Questions for Discussion

- The book of Jonah shows an extraordinary sense of magnanimity towards some of the most barbarous enemies of God's People. Are there other passages of the Bible which show the same generosity?

- Is bigotry an occupational hazard for all religions?

- Is being chosen by God a feather in one's cap, or a frightening burden?

# 10. On the Church's task:
## *to convert or to witness?*

What is the Church for? What is it meant to do? What is its task or mission in the world? What message is it supposed to preach to those of the human race who don't belong to the Church?

### *Once upon a time*

Once upon a time the Christian answer to these questions was quite straightforward. The Christian message was that complex of truths about God which had been revealed to us, and of which we Christians had the monopoly. I call them a 'complex', but they were really very simple. They could be summed up in a package any child could understand, the 'Penny Catechism'. As for conveying this message to others, this was simply a matter of instructing them in these truths. Whether they wanted them or not, whether they sounded more like Bad News than the Good News, was irrelevant. The Christian message was good for them, and that was all that mattered.

In such a view of *what* we had to preach, and *how* we preached it, there was little room for considering *whom* we were preaching it to. In fact we thought the question rather pointless. Young or old, first century or twenty-first, the important thing was that everybody should accept these truths, because those who did not were lost.

Catholic schools even made sure that the children knew them all by eleven, because at eleven plus they might go to non-Catholic schools.

## *What has changed?*

What has changed over recent years to make us feel that this analysis of 'what', 'who' and 'how' no longer does justice to the question? What has happened that Christians no longer see their mission in those terms? Certainly the different denominations no longer feel – *pace* the odd cranks – that it is their God-given vocation to demolish all others. But neither do Christians as a whole feel that this is how they would like to express their common mission to non-Christians. The conversion mentality we once all shared has become an ecumenism mentality and it has affected not only the way Christians regard each other, but the way they regard the whole non-Christian world. Why has this happened? What has changed?

Is it that the Christian message has changed? Is it that once we were absolutely certain what it was, and now we're no longer so sure? Have the age-old certainties we once boasted of been so diluted by the theologians that now we no longer know what to believe? Or is it that, in spite of everything, the gates of hell have prevailed, and we have given in to the spirit of the age, and our truths have become just as vague and woolly as everyone else's?

Or is it our contemporaries who have changed? Is it that people today, instead of welcoming dogma as they once did, simply refuse it and even resent it? Or is it that people today have been turned into such chaos by the psychologists that we no longer know how to address them? Or do we feel that the constantly accelerating speed of change has simply left us breathlessly and hopelessly behind?

Or is it neither the message itself, nor the public to whom we convey it, that has changed, but the way we convey it? Is it that, secretly, we still ultimately want to convert others, only it wouldn't do to say so, so we call it ecumenism? Or is it that we genuinely try to be ecumenical with our fellow

Christians, but simply cannot bring ourselves to feel the same towards these wretched non-Christians and non-believers, and the constant switching of masks is confusing us? Or is it that ecumenism has so changed our attitude to everyone that we're no longer sure of what the Church is for anyway, and whether we really want to preach anything to anyone?

What exactly has the Christian got to preach? What exactly is the Christian message?

## Christian message

If it is a collection of revealed truths, then all that the Christian can do is to preserve them intact, like a curator. Since the truths are eternal, fixed and unchangeable, people will either accept them or not, but that is all there is to it. They may change people's lives, but there is no question of the truths themselves undergoing any change. Christians may wish to brush the truths up from time to time, to ensure that they mean the same today as they meant yesterday. They may try to present them in a more attractive packaging, but that is a rather peripheral matter which can be left to the media experts. The icing on the cake. The Christian's real job is to pass on these truths from one generation to the next with the words, 'Come and share the treasure which I possess, because there is no truth or salvation outside of that'. For Jesus' command was explicit: 'Go and teach all nations, everyone everywhere, and get them to possess these truths as you possess them, otherwise they are lost.'

But supposing the Christian message and mission is not like that at all? Supposing the truth, whatever it is, is something no one can possess, because it is identified with God?

God is the mystery for which people will always strive, and yearn to be possessed by. But surely it is the height of blasphemy for any person, or any group, to imagine they can possess him, or make a corner of him! When Christians have turned to each other in the ecumenical dialogue, they have turned from saying, 'We own the divine truth, come and take it at our hands', to saying, 'We are unable to bear the divine truth creditably, come and help us'.

If this is the case, presumably the whole scenario changes. The Christian message is no longer a collection of truths of which Christians have a monopoly, but a vision of God through the eyes of Christ. The Christian has to say, 'I have seen what God is like in the life and teaching and death of this man. This has changed everything. I will never be able to see things the same way again. I have had to make a complete reappraisal of my attitudes, my suppositions, my expectations, my priorities. These have been turned upside down by what I now see my life is rooted in – the Father of our Lord Jesus Christ'.

### Who are the real believers?

Of course, Christians who express their faith in those terms lay themselves open to awkward questions. A friend of mine recently said to me, 'If you're redeemed as you say you are, why doesn't it show?' Nearer the knuckle, a South American priest has proposed that, in certain circumstances, the real believer in this modern age is the Marxist who rejects the world of corporate evil in the way that the New Testament rejects it – the *status quo* of exploitation and repression – and really believes in the possibility of a new world of justice and blessedness. In which case, of course, the real unbeliever, the real atheist, is the Christian who is quite willing to go along with the present unjust situation ('It's inevitable', 'It's natural', 'Nothing will ever change it'), and hopes eventually to escape from it into a supernatural fantasy, beyond death, where the tables will be turned.

Why would anyone call that 'unbelief'? Because Christians are supposed to believe in a God who fills the hungry with good things and sends the rich away empty; in a God whom they cannot see and therefore cannot love if they do not love the neighbour whom they can see; in a God who forbids them to offer their gift at the altar until they are reconciled with their brothers and sisters; in a God whose will must be done on earth as it is in heaven before the Kingdom can come. And if the Christian acts in a way quite contrary to such a belief, and does none of these things, and the Marxist does, who is the true believer? Jesus told a pointed parable about the son who promised to do what his father asked, and didn't, and the son who apparently refused, but then did it all the same.

The task of the Christian, to put it in the simplest possible terms, is to be a carbon copy of Jesus. It is by people doing just that, that Christianity has been passed on from age to age. This means that if, in the long run, a group of Christians is quite indistinguishable from the people around them, then it is difficult to see how they are conveying the Christian message to anyone. Sydney Carter puts the point in these words:

Your holy hearsay
is not evidence:
give me the good news
in the present tense.

What happened
nineteen hundred years ago
may not have happened:
how am I to know?

The living truth
is what I long to see:
I cannot lean upon
what used to be.

So shut the Bible up
and show me how
the Christ you talk about
is living now.
(In the Present Tense, from *The Two Way Clock,* Stainer &
Bell, 1969)

In other words, the Christian message is not preached by
pointing back to the eternal truth revealed 1900 years ago.
What people want to know is whether Christ is still alive
now. And how can they know that outside of our lives?

Another *cri-de-coeur* has put it this way:

Don't need no god.
Don't need no eternal paternal god.
Don't need no reassuringly protective
                good and evil in perspective – god.
 Don't need no imported distorted
                inflated updated
                holy roller, save your soul, or
                anaesthetisingly opiate – gods.
Don't need no 'all creatures that on earth do dwell'
                be good or you go to hell - god.
Don't need no Hare Krishna Hare Krishna
                Hail Mary Hail Mary - god.
Don't need no god.
I need human beings.
I need some kind
of love.
I need you.
(A. Darlington, *The Ecologist,* Nov. 1974, p.335)

Is this mere humanism? Was God guilty of the same mere
humanism when he embodied his message in the love that a
man showed to all who came his way?

## Key texts

This chapter may seem to have oversimplified things by being very selective about the Gospel texts quoted. The texts have indeed been selected carefully. But then they are the key texts, the ones which govern the way the rest are to be understood. The Great Commission to go and teach all nations must not be allowed to sabotage the Great Command, which is to go and love them.

The Christian mission is not primarily to proselytise, to control, to lay down the law, to overcome all opposition, to subjugate, to build up an empire, to outshine everyone else. The Church is not primarily a fortress embattled against the world, or a sanctuary for those who cannot cope with the world. The Church is primarily a 'sign' to the world, a sacrament of Christ, as Christ is a sacrament of God. If the Church cannot mediate to people the love of God which was made visible in the life of Christ, then it has lost the reason for its existence.

Jesus forbade his disciples to lord it over other people: they had to serve them as he did. In fact, the one positive commandment he gave them was to love others in the way he had loved them, because that was the only way people could experience a God who is defineed as Love. This would crucify them, as it did him. But this was the only way people would ever have of telling whether these really were disciples of his. In the last analysis, this would be the only criterion on which judgement would be passed. People would not be asked whether they wore the right label, or like the Samaritan heretic the wrong label, or even whether they wore no label at all. They would simply be asked, 'Did you show love to your brothers and sisters?' If you didn't, it would be silly to call yourself a follower of Jesus. Good gracious! You couldn't even call yourself someone who knows God.

In effect, therefore, Jesus' message was that the Kingdom

of God comes into being wherever and whenever people love each other, and accept one another's burden in a spirit of concern and compassion, of sensitivity and generosity. To that Kingdom all people are called, because that is the apple of God's eye. But why should anyone imagine that all people are called to the Church, which exists simply to bear witness to that Kingdom?

Jesus did not tell his disciples to work for the Church. He told them to work for God's Kingdom – the glorious future when the whole community of the human race would be one in love. He didn't tell them to convert others to believe what they believed. More important was to help them grow in love, and to be at their service to make that possible.

That is a simple enough agenda. The implications, of course, are infinite.

## Questions for Discussion

- 'In the spirit of the age, our Christian truths have become just as vague and woolly as everyone else's.' Are there good grounds for this accusation?

- 'A Church which cannot mediate to people the love of God made visible in the life of Christ has lost the reason for its existence.' Do you agree?

- 'All people are called to build God's Kingdom. Not all people are called to the Church, which exists simply to bear witness to that Kingdom.' How 'evangelical' do you think the Church ought to be?

# 11. On forgiveness:
## *what about God's wrath?*

Everyone knows the Gospel story of the wretched woman caught in the act of adultery. The traditional punishment was stoning. Jesus, invited to adjudicate, suggested that the first stone be thrown by a guiltless person. There were no takers (John 8:1-11).

Fewer people know the parallel story in the Old Testament of the wretched man caught gathering wood on the sabbath. When God is asked to adjudicate, he decrees death by stoning, and the whole community is invited to take part (Numbers 15:32-36). At an Anglican evensong I attended, the two stories were appointed as the readings for the day. I presume they were deliberately chosen to form a contrast. In both cases, someone has to face an angry crowd armed with stones. Under orders from God, one is spared and the other comes to a sticky end.

## *Two images of God*

What worried me was the implication that the contrast was between the God of the Old Testament and the God of the New Testament. It was as if in the Old Testament God was stern, just and unforgiving, but in the New Testament forgiving, merciful and gentle. This is, of course, ridiculously untrue. Anyone looking for the Bible's most ruthless and pitiless texts would probably need to go to the New Testament pages of Paul and Revelation. Anyone looking for its most tender and loving pages would probably find them in the Old Testament psalms and the Song of Songs.

By sheer chance, the psalm appointed for that Sunday

evensong was the highly moving Psalm [102] 103, with its consoling words:

> Bless the Lord, O my soul...
> and forget not all his benefits,
> who forgives all your iniquity...
> The Lord is merciful and gracious...
> He does not deal with us according to our sins...
> For as the heavens are high above the earth,
> so great is his steadfast love...
> as far as the east is from the west,
> so far does he remove our sins.

The Old Testament is quite as convinced as the New that, in the last analysis, God is not a wrathful avenger threatening punishment. He does not hold our sins against us. He will not give us our deserts.

I remember the psalm being quoted most aptly when I was on study leave in Jerusalem the year Willi Brandt, then German Chancellor, paid his first visit to Israel as a token of reparation for the Nazi atrocities in World War II. Standing in Yad Vashem, the memorial to the six million victims of the concentration camps, he recited the Jewish prayer as an implicit plea for Jewish forgiveness:

> The Lord is merciful and gracious...
> He will not keep his anger for ever.
> He does not deal with us according to our sins...
> He removes our sins. He forgives. He forgets.

Outside the memorial a crowd of protesters paraded with banners proclaiming, 'We will not forget', 'We will not forgive'.

If God were as unforgiving as people are! Winston Churchill once said of an unyielding colleague, 'There but for the grace of God goes God.' A notice-board outside a convent building reads, 'Trespassers will be prosecuted with the full rigour of the law. Signed, Sisters of Mercy'. Thank

God the mercy of God really is mercy, because if he marked our iniquities, who could stand? Who would survive? And that is a comment of the Old Testament, not the New. Its pages portray a loving and forgiving God as boldly as any page of the New Testament.

The contrast between the two evensong readings, therefore, is not between the Old Testament and the New, but between two images of God. One image is of an angry, stern and threatening God. The other is of a God who loves, forgives, and accepts. Both images are to be found in the Old Testament and the New. Both can even be found together in one and the same passage (see Hosea 11:1-9). At different times and in different circumstances, either image may be in our mind to represent for us what God is like. The question is, which of the two images is determinative? Which of the two finally predominates? What kind of God do we ultimately believe in?

### God the mother

I am writing this from Norwich, where we venerate a medieval hermit saint known as Mother Julian, who is unique not only for her visions, but for breaking into the male world of publishing as early as the fourteenth century. There is no question of which image of God she puts uppermost. Her visions show her a God who is so loving, tender-hearted and forgiving that the word 'Mother' ought to be used rather than 'Father'. Her most well-known saying, which she repeats often, runs:

> All shall be well,
> And all shall be well,
> And all manner of thing shall be well.

She is convinced that in the last analysis, however, unlikely it may sound, what will ultimately triumph is goodness, not evil. Why should she be so confident? Because the Gospel has assured her that reality is not rooted in chance or meaninglessness, but in a God who can only be defined as love, acceptance and forgiveness. If the rock foundation on which all things stand, the soil in which all things are rooted, is to be seen as ultimately loving, how can the world's story fail to turn out well?

> Wouldst thou witten the Lord's meaning in this thing? Learn it well: love was his meaning. Who shewed it thee? Love. What shewed he thee? Love. Wherefore shewed it he? For love. Hold thee therein, and thou shalt learn and know more in the same… Ere God made us he loved us; which love was never slacked nor ever shall be. And in this love he hath done all his works; and in this love he hath made all things profitable to us; and in this love our life is everlasting.
> (*Revelations of Divine Love,* Methuen 1958, chapter 86.)

Julian repeats this conviction of hers most insistently when she deals with the problem of evil. Given the reality of sin and evil in the world, how can it be true to say that all things will ultimately be well? Undeterred, she assures herself that in the long run even sin will fit into the pattern. 'Sin is behovable', she says, meaning useful. That is to say, sin is not useless. Sin is not unable to be integrated by God into that plan of his in which all things will be well. Sin must not be given priority over the more fundamental reality of God's love, which she is confident must ultimately triumph, even over evil.

## *Insight*

She did not come to this conclusion lightly. The problem of evil nags her, and she returns to it again, particularly in the light of the official teaching of the Church. According to this teaching, all shall not be well for some people. All manner of thing shall be awful. In the long run many people will not find union with God, but will be separated from him for ever. The unrepentant and the unbaptised, for example. The Jews in particular, who have explicitly rejected the Christian revelation, will go to hell. All medieval theologians agreed on this.

At midpoint in her Revelations, Julian struggles and agonises over the problem. On the one hand she is desperate to remain a true daughter of the Church. On the other hand she is determined not to abandon her basic insight. She portrays the struggle eloquently:

> Part of our belief is that many creatures will be damned; for example, the angels who fell from heaven through pride, and are now fiends; and those men on earth who die apart from the Faith of Holy Church, namely the heathen; and those too, who are christened but live unchristian lives, and so die out of love – all these shall be condemned to hell everlastingly, as Holy Church teaches me to believe. This being so I thought it quite impossible that everything should turn out well, as our Lord was now showing me. I had no answer to this revelation save this: 'What is impossible to you is not impossible to me. I shall honour my word in every respect, and I will make everything turn out for the best.' Thus was I taught by God's grace to hold steadfastly to the faith I had already learned, but at the same time to believe quite seriously that everything *would* turn out all right, as our Lord was showing…
>
> The revelation was one of goodness, with very little reference to evil. I was not drawn thereby from any article of the Faith in which Holy Church teaches me to believe … But I did not see the Jews specifically mentioned as those who did him to death. (Only) by my Faith I knew that they were accursed and eternally damned…
>
> God has shown the very great pleasure given him by all those men and women who wholeheartedly, humbly and willingly, receive the preaching and teaching of Holy

Church. For it is *his* Holy Church. He is its foundation, its being, its teaching. He is its teacher, and the end and the reward for which every normal soul is striving...

(But what I *saw* was) that God does everything. I saw no sin, and I saw that everything was all right. And it was when God showed me sin that he said, 'Everything is going to be all right.'

*(Revelations of Divine Love,* Penguin 1966, chapters 32-34.)

Julian is engaged in a struggle between two levels of faith, between what she had been told was true and what she knew in her bones was true; between a particular theology and an insight, a vision. What she had seen was hell itself. What she had seen, even in the midst of hell, was that all shall be well. What she had seen was that 'there may be no *wrath* in God'. She repeats this phrase ten times.

The Penguin editor and translator of her visions concludes that Julian was rather naïve. Her optimism was a piece of wishful thinking, in flat contradiction to the teaching of the Church. She had fallen into heresy, poor thing. She had done it from the best of motives, of course. But being cloistered she was a bit simple: she had never encountered the sort of evil which deserves God's anger and condemnation.

Julian had said that there was no wrath in God, but there was wrath in me as I read such a patronising appraisal of someone whose little finger is thicker than any commentator's thigh.

## A forgiving God

No, Julian was a woman of insight, and the insight was centuries ahead of the theology of her time. One can only admire the tenacity and courage with which she clung to her insight in the face of an official theology which could find no room for it.

In the face of two images of God, she insists, one has to be primary and determinative. And what she found at the heart of the Gospel is a God who does not threaten retribution, condemnation and punishment, but a God who simply forgives over and over again. When Peter asked whether it was sufficient to forgive someone seven times over for the same offence (a generous offer), he was told that seventy times seven times would not be enough: God is even more forgiving. Whatever anyone has done, it does not earn God's condemnation, only his forgiveness. His attitude will never be one of reproof or disapproval or condemnation, only pity. 'Neither do I condemn you; go, and do not sin again.'

At the heart of the Gospel stands the cross. On that cross, the Son of God does not blast his executioners to hell, but forgives them. And he is so much his father's son that we have to understand that God is like that. Those who accept this will find their lives revolutionised.

The notice-board standing outside the gates of Paradise reads: 'Trespassers will be forgiven.' That is what heaven is all about. A famous epitaph reads:

Here lies Martin Elginbrodde;
have mercy on my soul, Lord God,
as I would do were I Lord God
and you were Martin Elginbrodde.

If we can be as forgiving as that, could God in any way be less forgiving?

If that insight into God is primary and determinative, then we shall have to re-think the texts, in the New Testament as well as the Old, which speak of an angry, vengeful and punishing God. Shall we dismiss them as a primitive strand of revelation, a sub-Christian fossil which the fullness of Christian revelation has superseded? Or would that be too arbitrarily selective of the texts we take seriously? Shall we be bolder, like the fourth Gospel, and turn the texts into a revelation of the wrathfulness and condemnation that lies deep in ourselves if we turn our backs on God? Or shall we be bolder still and recognise the language as metaphorical, not literal, since it is literally incompatible with a God who continues throughout to be total forgiveness? How else can limited human language express the seriousness of God's love, and his passionate concern for the wellbeing of those whom sin would enslave, dehumanise and destroy?

People must decide for themselves how to interpret the Bible's vengeful texts. What is clear is that, as they stand, they make nonsense of the texts which speak of God's love. Forgiveness simply is not forgiveness if it is hiding a big stick for emergency use.

Mother Julian made up her mind quite firmly. She put her money on the God of love and mercy, in the conviction that this love can overcome even the worst of sins, and far more effectively than wrath. The God of wrath simply does not exist. Whether we welcome him or reject him, God will meet each of us with utter love, and there is nothing we can do that will change this attitude of his.

'In God there may be no wrath.' 'All shall be well.' 'Neither do I condemn you.' What a consoling message! 'Now go, and do likewise.' What a frightening message!

## Questions for Discussion

- Find some of the ruthless New Testament texts, and some of the tender Old Testament passages, referred to at the beginning of this chapter.

- Was Julian of Norwich being naïve in insisting that in the long run 'all manner of thing shall be well'?

- Four ways of interpreting the Bible's vengeful texts are suggested above. Which (if any) makes best sense? Can you suggest others?

# 12. On being perfect:
## *a command or only an ideal?*

Everyone has a rough idea of the contents of the Sermon on the Mount (Matthew 5-7). The quotations trip easily off the tongue: the salt of the earth, the light of the world, loving your enemies, turning the other cheek, not blowing your own trumpet, serving God and Mammon, the birds of the air and the lilies of the field – not to mention the clarion call of the Beatitudes with which the whole sermon starts: 'Blessed are the poor'.

What is the pattern and rationale behind these quotations? What is the main point of this preaching of Jesus? Is he proposing this teaching as a law, or only as a counsel of perfection? Is it meant to be a realistic programme for action or only a utopian ideal?

Perhaps we should start by clearing the ground, and eliminating some approaches to the Sermon which are unhelpful.

### *New Testament versus Old?*

One of the most popular ways of introducing the Sermon is to turn it into an attack on the Old Testament in general, and on Judaism in particular. So in commentary after commentary the Sermon is hailed as:

'The New Era of Love versus the Old Era of Law'
'The Mountain of Peace versus the Mountain of Wrath'
'The Spirit versus the Letter'
'True Religion of the Heart versus Superficial Legalism',

and so on.

No doubt the authors who thought up these titles are deadly serious, but there is a touch of zany humour about such pontifical words. For a perfect example of heartless legalism, one would not turn to a Jewish author but to a Christian moralist, liturgist or canon lawyer. No one has yet been able to outdo them.

In actual fact the Sermon on the Mount closely echoes the Old Testament. Indeed, Matthew's whole purpose would be frustrated if his readers didn't spot this straight away. He sees Jesus as a new Moses, and deliberately composes his Gospel in five parts in imitation of the five books of Moses. When he represents Jesus teaching on a mountainside (Luke's teaching is given on a plain), readers are inevitably reminded of Moses on Mount Sinai. But the scene is meant to reinforce the teaching of Moses, not to countermand it. 'I have come,' says Matthew's Jesus, 'not to abolish the Old Testament, but to fulfil it.' Not an iota, not a single dot of it is to fall away. It is as permanent as the heavens, and Jesus has come to confirm it (see Matthew 5:17-18).

The Sermon on the Mount is full of quotations from the psalms, from the prophets, even from rabbinical writings. There is no phrase in these three chapters for which a Jewish parallel cannot be found. That's why it is absurd to use the Sermon in order to belittle the Old Testament, when it is meant to be an echo of all its finest insights. According to Matthew, Jesus' aim is not to replace the Old Testament with something different, but to bring to perfection something that was already good and beautiful. The stained glass New Testament evangelists in Chartres cathedral are shown as sitting on the shoulders of the Old Testament prophets. That makes Matthew's point exactly.

## A new law?

How does Jesus bring the Old Testament to perfection? Is it by updating the old law and extending it? When Jesus says,

'Unless your righteousness exceeds that of the Scribes and Pharisees', does he mean that they haven't taken the law seriously enough, and that he insists on pushing it to its logical conclusion? So that where previously murder was prohibited, Jesus adds, 'So is hatred'; and where previously adultery was forbidden, Jesus adds, 'So are bad thoughts'? Is the Sermon on the Mount a series of laws adding codicils to the Old Testament?

There are many who interpret the Sermon in this way. They have produced a Christianity as preposterous as the hilarious setting of the Highway Code to Anglican Chant by the Mastersingers (Parlophone R5428). We laugh not because we think all codes are crazy, or all hymns ludicrous, but because of the combination of the two. People cannot be made good by Act of Parliament.

We may object that the Old Testament Jews kept turning their religion into a system of law-keeping. Perhaps, but then so have Christians, and very successfully, ever since. I can quote chapter and verse. Jesus told his disciples to love their enemies and do good to those who hated them. The manual from which I learnt my moral theology in the 1940s took this as a law, and assured me that such a law did not demand that I offer pardon to my enemy before he asked for it!

I read about a Jewish woman in a German concentration camp who witnessed an SS man drown a new-born baby under a tap with the words, 'Here you go, little Moses'. But she then fought to protect the baby of a German woman being attacked by the released prisoners. Is that closer to Jesus' meaning?

More eloquent still is the anonymous Prayer from a Concentration Camp, which runs:

> Peace to all men of evil will! Let there be an end to all vengeance, to all demands for punishment and retribution. There are too many martyrs...

We beseech you, Lord, weigh not their sufferings on the scales of thy justice, and lay not these sufferings to the torturers' charge, to exact a terrible reckoning from them. Pay them back in a different way. Put down in favour of the executioners and informers and traitors and all men of evil will – the courage of the others, their humility, their lofty dignity, their constant inner striving and invincible hope, their love, their ravaged broken hearts that remained steadfast and confident in the face of death itself, yes, even at moments of utmost weakness…

Let all of this, O Lord, be laid before thee for the forgiveness of sins, as a ransom for the triumph of righteousness. Let the good and not the evil be taken into account.

And may we remain in our enemies' memory not as their victims, not as a nightmare, not as haunting spectres, but as helpers in their striving to destroy the fury of their criminal passions. There is nothing more that we want of them. Peace to all men of evil will!

Or the Muslim prayer:

O Lord, I beseech you,
make me thankful for the grace you have given me.
As for those who persecute me in the name of religion,
thinking they are doing your will,
pardon them, in your mercy.
For if you had revealed to them what you have revealed to me,
they would not be acting as they are.
And if you had hidden from me what you have hidden from them,
I might have been the persecutor instead of the persecuted.
Glory to you in all that you do.
Glory to you in all that you will.

Is this perhaps more like what Jesus meant?

The law requires only the minimum. Jesus demanded the very opposite when he asked his audience to treat enemies exactly as God does, making no distinction between enemy and friend. Jesus wants to base his life on a vision where law is simply irrelevant. Jesus said he had come to bring the law to its fulfilment. He had come to draw attention again and again to its original purpose for those who keep thinking that law tells you how to serve God without loving him.

## Counsels of perfection?

Is such a programme realistic? Can people meet the requirements of a love which is so open-ended? Surely such perfection is designed only for the few, not for the many?

Many people are beguiled by this line of reasoning. When they analyse the Sermon and discover it is not a law binding on everyone, they conclude it must be a 'counsel of perfection' designed for the élite.

According to this theology there are two classes of Christians, tourist and first. The tourist class comprises the bulk of the membership. Their job is to keep the commandments. They cannot reach their destination without. But if people want to travel first class, and arrive more surely and with clean hands, they must pay more. Very few can afford to do so – bishops, priests, those in religious life, and perhaps the very occasional unmarried layperson. (See Thomas Aquinas, *Summa Theologiae*, Q. 107-8.)

For those who follow this convenient line of thinking, the teaching of Jesus becomes a series of pious admonitions, with no obligation attached. The Sermon on the Mount becomes an advanced course, an optional extra for those who have already passed the ordinary course of the Ten Commandments. Ordinary tourist Christians are not obliged to be poor, meek, humble, merciful and clean of heart – that is for the professionals. They're not bound to suppress anger, or offer no resistance, or be so truthful that oaths are unnecessary – that is for the holy people. They're not committed to love their enemies, or to refuse to be worried about food and clothing, or to take up the cross daily – that is for priests and nuns. They absolve the rest of us from these arduous tasks. They are doing it for us.

This travesty of the New Testament still features regularly in many sermons and in countless books of spiritual advice. I call it a travesty because Jesus made no distinction between what he demanded of his immediate disciples and what he asked of any follower of his. He did indeed counsel perfection, but he proposed it for everyone. Those who are unwilling to accept his way of life as a programme, however poorly they perform, ought not to call themselves followers of his. Thank goodness Vatican II spelled this out in plain terms, making it impossible, one would hope, ever to return to the idea of perfection only for the élite.

## An ideal?

If the Sermon then is not a series of counsels of perfection for the élite, but a programme of action for everyone, why not come clean and call it a law?

The answer is easy. Because the keeping of a law can never put anyone in the right relationship with God. The bond which unites God to people, and people to God, is love not law. The demands of law can always be met, and if necessary a receipt issued to vouch for the fact. The demands of love can never be met, because love is always on the lookout for further opportunities to express itself. A State Registered Nurse can lay aside her concern for her patient once her eight hours are up. But a mother must care for her sick child day and night, as long as the child needs her. One is bound by law, the other by love.

What title, then, should we give to the Sermon on the Mount? Perhaps a description would be easier than a definition. The Sermon is Jesus' attempt to explain what right relationship with God consists of, and has always consisted of, though people keep getting it wrong.

Of course, it could be objected that people keep getting it wrong because it is totally unrealistic. How can flesh and blood accept an invitation to be as perfect as God? What mere human being can measure up to such other-worldly idealism? All very well for God to say he's made us a little lower than the gods: we're willing to settle for being a little above the Joneses!

This pessimistic approach to perfection is at the heart of many stories:

> Moishe dies and is admitted into heaven. As God goes off to prepare something to eat, he tells Moishe to turn on the TV to see what is going on in the other place. Orgy after orgy! Moishe wets his lips. Eventually God returns with a sardine sandwich. Moishe protests. What is going on? God explains: 'Moishe, for the two of us, it was hardly worth cooking.'

> Only those with no brothers dream of all men being brothers. (Anon)

> Jesus saved the world? What was it like before? (P. De Rosa)

> Good resolutions are useless attempts to interfere with scientific laws. (Oscar Wilde)

There is nothing new, of course, about such protests that Jesus is demanding the impossible. His disciples made exactly the same objection in a similar context. Jesus' reply is famous: 'For man this is impossible; for God all things are possible' (Matthew 19:26). A human being like us in all things – weak, groping, uncertain, learning by experience – Jesus lived out this programme in the power of the Spirit poured into him by the Father, and assured Christians they can do the same, in the power of the same Spirit poured into their hearts. God intends to bring all mankind to the perfection expressed here. It will always be God's will that all people should aim at this.

## *The heart of the matter*

Of all the teachings of Jesus in the Sermon on the Mount, which is the central one governing all the rest? What is at the heart of the matter?

Personally, I find that among all the thoughts expressed in Matthew 5-7, none is finally as basic and far-reaching as the words on retaliation. Jesus says:

> You have often heard the law given to our ancestors:
> 'You must love your fellow countryman',
> as much as to say, 'You may hate your enemy.'
> But I say this:
> It's when they hate you, you must love them,
> and when they wrong you, go be kind to them;
> when they curse you, you must bless them,
> and when they hurt you, speak to God for them:
>> He makes his sun shine on good and bad alike,
>> his gentle rain falls on saints and sinners.
> If you love only those who love you,
> if you're kind only to those who are kind to you,
> if you lend only to those who'll help you,
> you're only paying for what they give to you.
>> He makes his sun shine on good and bad alike,
>> his gentle rain falls on saints and sinners.
> It's those who hate you, you must love and tend,
> to those who wrong you, go, be kind and lend,
> without expecting any dividend,
> except to be just like God in the end.
>> He makes his sun shine on good and bad alike,
>> his gentle rain falls on saints and sinners.
> You must be perfect as your Father is,
> and have compassion as your Father has.
> He's kind to those who never thank him,
> he's good to those who have no time for him.
>> He makes his sun shine on good and bad alike,
>> his gentle rain falls on saints and sinners.

(Matthew 5:44-48, tr. H. J. Richards, *The Gospel in Song,* Kevin Mayhew 1983)

These words are dynamite. Those who understand them have found their lives turned upside down. Why? Because the most natural thing in the world, when you are attacked or challenged, is to resist, to retaliate, to hit back, to distinguish carefully between those we can safely give ourselves to, and those who would take advantage of us. As Ernest Bevin retorted (when Emmanuel Shinwell said of a colleague, 'He's his own worst enemy'), 'Not while I'm alive.'

Jesus is saying that true religion, true relationship with God, means going in exactly the opposite direction. That alone makes us like God. 'Be ye perfect' does not mean 'Do the impossible', but quite simply, 'Be like God, otherwise you're wasting your time. Be like God, putting *no* limit on your loving, as God doesn't.'

God's love for people is free, open, always available, and undiscriminating. He makes no distinction between friends and enemies. His sun shines on both. He allows himself to be taken advantage of. That is what the word 'God' is all about. It is only total love of that kind that can transform the world, and save it from being overcome by evil.

To take any other attitude, to retaliate, is in fact to give evil the upper hand. Before, there was only one under the control of evil: now there are two. Evil propagates itself in this way, like a contagious disease. Those who keep taking an eye for an eye will eventually turn the whole world blind.

Evil can only be contained and defeated by absorbing it, by neutralising it with love. Those whom we love have thereby ceased being our enemies: it is as simple as that.

It is that kind of love, when it is exercised by people, that is the active presence of God in the world. Those who refuse to love like that are refusing to open their part of the world to the presence of God, because it is only through people's lives that God can be made present. Sydney Carter wrote these lines on the godly work of Mother Teresa. It can stand as a tribute to the millions of people, Christian and non-Christian, who day by day make God's love real:

> No revolution will come in time
> to alter this man's life
> except the one
> surprise of being loved.
>
> He has no interest in Civil Rights,
> neo-Marxism,
> psychiatry,
> or any kind of sex.
>
> He has only twelve more hours to live,
> so never mind about
> a cure for cancer, smoking, leprosy
> or osteo-arthritis.
>
> Over this dead loss to society
> you pour your precious ointment,
> call the bluff
> and laugh at the
>
> Fat and clock-faced gravity
> of our economy.
> You wash the feet
> that will not walk tomorrow.
>
> Come, levity of love,
> show him, show me,
> in this
> last step of time
>
> Eternity,
> leaping and capering.
> (Stainer & Bell, 1972)

## In the spirit of Christ

I have suggested that certain approaches to the Sermon on the Mount are misleading, and can in fact be positively harmful. The Sermon is not a diatribe against the Old Testament: it reflects all that is best in its writings. The Sermon is not a code of extra laws added on top of existing laws: people cannot be made good by Act of Parliament. The Sermon is not a series of counsels addressed to an élite: it is addressed to every person of good will.

What, then, is left? An ideal, a series of illustrations of what religion is most deeply about. To this ideal all people are called, with the assurance that in the Spirit of Christ it is a practical proposition. And at its centre stands a God-like love, which alone is able to transform the world into the Kingdom of God.

The Sermon ends with words, 'It is not those who are able to say, *Lord, Lord,* (or *Kyrie, Kyrie,*) who will enter the Kingdom, but those who do the will of God, even if they have never heard the word *Kyrie* (see Matthew 7:21). In other words, it is no good saying, when it comes to the crunch, 'But Lord, I'm a Christian'. The reply will be, 'I don't care if you're a chrysanthemum. Did you try to do the will of God as expressed in the Sermon on the Mount? Were those the values that governed your life?'

## Questions for Discussion

• The law can only demand the minimum. Jesus' teaching demands the maximum. Surely this is unrealistic?

• 'A healthy appetite for righteousness, kept in due control by good manners, is an excellent thing. But to *hunger and thirst* after it is often merely a symptom of spiritual diabetes.' (C. D. Broad) How far do you agree?

- 'The Sermon on the Mount describes a society in which people relate to each other in a God-like love. Such a society does not yet exist, and even our best efforts can be no more than compromises.' (Bishop R. Harries) Do we compromise too easily?

# 13. On faith:
## *certainty or uncertainty?*

Faith is a reality which it is surprisingly difficult to analyse. We use the word 'faith', and words related to it (like faithful and fidelity, belief and believer, creed and credence), with an extraordinary variety of meanings, ranging from a rocklike certainty at one end of the spectrum to complete uncertainty at the other.

### *Spectrum*

At one end of this spectrum, 'I believe' can mean 'I am utterly convinced and certain.' In this sense it denotes a total trust and confidence in one's object of belief or faith: 'I believe in democracy', 'I believe in the Labour Party', 'I believe in Volkswagens'.

If the word is used in a religious context, faith tends to refer to the truths or convictions upon which a religion is based. The question, 'What is your faith?' means, 'What is your religion?' And people will reply, 'I am of the Muslim faith', 'I am of the Jewish faith'. So Christians will speak of the Faith of Our Fathers, Handing on the Faith, Believers and Non-Believers, the Apostles' Creed, and so on.

But once a faith is defined in terms of a list of propositions which are accepted because they come from God, a number of difficulties begin to arise. Is this list to be thought of as continually being added to? So that the faith of Isaiah in 700BC was necessarily more complex than the faith of Abraham a thousand years earlier? Wouldn't that be odd? And odder still to imagine that what today's Christian believes in is somehow more than what Matthew, Mark, Luke and John believed in?

What is even more worrying is that, as the creeds of different people disagree with each other at more and more points, what was once held as absolutely certain has to become more and more uncertain, however loudly it continues to be proclaimed. The disagreeing creeds can't all be right. Alexander Pope's comment is apt:

> For forms of government let fools contest;
> whate'er is best administered is best.
> For modes of faith let graceless zealots fight;
> His can't be wrong whose life is in the right.
> In faith and hope the world will disagree,
> but all mankind's concern is charity.
> (*Essay on Man,* 3, 303)

So faith slowly becomes enveloped in a mist of uncertainty. What is believed continues to be held firmly enough, but less firmly than what can be seen, or tasted, or touched, or arrived at by reason. The object of faith is somehow less solid than the object of scientific investigation. One believes only what one unfortunately cannot prove.

Gradually faith has dwindled from a divine obligation to a simple option. People may believe or not – it is their free choice. 'Do you believe in God?' 'Do you believe in ghosts?' 'Do you believe in women's lib?' Roget's *Thesaurus* lists the word 'faith' alongside the words 'credence', 'opinion', 'surmise', 'distinct impression'. People say, 'I do believe it is going to rain'. A true-to-life stage clergyman says, 'Almighty God tells us in the book of Isaiah, and I believe he says it with some degree of justification...'

Even as a religious word, faith has by this time become rather suspect. It is something indulged in by people with religious inclinations, not by normal people. There is more than a suspicion that it provides them with a useful escape hatch out of the cruel real world. Mercifully for them, the world of faith cannot be disproved. But in the last analysis faith has become synonymous with naïvety, childish credulity, and gullibility.

We have run the word 'faith' through a considerable gamut. Dozens of other illustrations could have been used. These examples are perhaps sufficient to establish the fact that the word is used in a wide variety of senses, and can cover both what is most sacred and certain, and what is entirely uncertain and optional. In what sense does the Bible use the word?

## Faith as certainty

Perhaps the first thing that should be noted about the biblical use of the word 'faith' is its personal character. People with faith do not simply believe 'that'; they believe 'in'. They do not simply accept a series of propositions that can be listed as a creed. They accept a person.

Faith, therefore, is never as academic, abstract and theoretical as we have made it in our language. It does not simply involve the mind; it involves the whole person committing himself or herself to another. And when that other is God, the word 'faith' defines the ideal relationship between people and God.

To believe in God, in biblical language, means to acknowledge his utter and undisputed sovereignty, to stand before him knowing that he is the source of all that one has and is, and to be totally open to his love and his demands. It means to stop relying on one's own strength, on one's own independent way of thinking, in order to rely entirely on the word and power of God.

To believe is to 'hear', 'obey', 'follow', 'come to', 'welcome', 'abide in', 'know' (in the way husbands and wives 'know' each other). These are the words which the Bible puts in parallel with the word 'faith', all verbs rather than nouns. Faith is never something that people have; it is something that they do. It is never a mere academic exercise in which the mind assents to certain articles of belief; it is an exercise in which the whole person commits herself or himself to God. In this sense, it is scarcely distinguishable from hope and love.

To say that faith of this kind 'saves' people (as the Bible does repeatedly: see Genesis 15:6, Romans 4:3, Galatians 3:6, James 2:23, Hebrews 11:12) does not mean that people do something so pleasing to God that he rewards them. It simply means that those who adopt such an attitude of confidence, hope and love are entirely open for God to do his work in them. It means that such an all-embracing, hopeful and loving faith puts them in the right relationship with God, and that is salvation.

Yet the basic connotation of 'faith' remains one of certainty. It is rooted in the Hebrew word *emeth,* which means firmness, solidarity, reliability and dependability. God is *emeth* – rock-solid. The appropriate response to such a reality is utter confidence that one will never be let down. This confidence is expressed in the related word *Amen. Amen* means 'That is for sure'. Whatever the difficulty, however much things seem to point in the opposite direction, 'I believe' means 'I stake my life on God, as ultimately the only reality which is utterly dependable'.

## A pilgrimage of faith

Taking up this theme of certainty, it is easy enough to tell the story of the Old Testament as a pilgrimage of faith. Any biblical wordbook or dictionary will provide such an outline under the word 'faith'.

At the head of the procession stands Abraham, the prototype of faith and father of all the faithful. His story is told in the book of Genesis as a deliberate contrast with the story of Adam. Adam was the closed man, the man of un-faith.

Abraham is a man unconditionally open to God, as the three highlights of his story are meant to illustrate. When God's word calls him, he leaves everything and goes out into only God knows where. It is similarly God's word alone which ensures that a son is born to him, against all human likelihood. And when the same word of God demands that the son be given back, he is ready to sacrifice his whole future and put his trust only in the God who can bring life out of death.

So the Bible establishes what the word 'faith' is to mean for the rest of the story. It means complete availability of this kind, for this alone can be 'reckoned as righteousness' (Genesis 15:6), that is, demonstrate a right relationship with God. Such faith will make countless thousands point back to Abraham as their father. Such faith makes his story a proclamation of the Gospel even before the coming of Christ (Galatians 3:8).

The Exodus story which follows is the Abraham story writ large. Israel as a nation is called to travel the road that Abraham travelled, and to discover the reliability of her God. In the escape from Egypt, in the long desert journey, and especially in the covenant at Mount Sinai, Israel's faith was born, and she celebrated that faith in terms of these events ever after.

Not that there were no hazards to be overcome. The story of the desert journey is punctuated with the grumbling of a people on the march, and their leader Moses has as many struggles as Abraham had, before he succeeds in planting the faith born at Sinai in the soil of the Promised Land. And even there Israel's faith remained in crisis, with new circumstances, new problems and new gods constantly threatening to distort or even to stifle the fragile relationship which Israel had established with God. It was time for prophets to arise.

The prophets were the salvation of Israel. Each of them a reincarnation of Moses, as it were, they laboured to build up in Samaria and Jerusalem the faith that had sustained Israel on her desert march. The prophets were the conscience of Israel, crying out ceaselessly against any compromise with the present which would betray the past, against any formalism which would institutionalise the living God, and against any attempt to find security in anything other than God. The repeated disasters recounted in the books of Kings (hunger and want, invasion and defeat, schism and exile) – all these, they said, were due to a lack of faith. Strong faith would have brought stability, prosperity and peace. Isaiah sums up the prophetic message:

> Open the gates,
> that the righteous nation which keeps *faith*
> may enter in.
> Thou dost keep him in perfect peace,
> whose mind is *stayed* on thee,
> because he *trusts* in thee.
> *Trust* in the Lord for ever,
> for the Lord God
> Is an everlasting rock.
> (Isaiah 26:2-4)

> If you will not *believe,*
> surely you shall not be established.
> (Isaiah 7:9)

Or more succinctly (for the phrase plays on the word *emeth*):

> If you do not say Amen to me,
> you can say Amen.
> (trans. H. J. Richards)

It is the occupational hazard of a prophet to be pessimistic. The pages of the Israelite prophets are full of complaints about the weak and uncertain faith of the many, and about the disastrous consequences such unfaithfulness must bring. Yet they speak more hopefully, here and there, of an inner

Israel, a 'remnant' which remains steadfast and faithful. And they all look forward to a future when the faith of this remnant will be vindicated, a future when God will reveal himself openly and show himself to be what Israel's faith has always proclaimed him to be, a future when all people will be able to put their unqualified confidence in the Lord.

The New Testament announces that this prophetic hope was fulfilled in Jesus of Nazareth. He is the Lord who makes God's presence totally available, and who removes all uncertainty. To believe in him is to be saved. To refuse belief is to be damned. The pilgrimage of faith has reached its goal.

## Faith as uncertainty

The classical presentation of the theme of faith outlined above has a pleasing consistency. By concentrating entirely on the certainty of faith, and by showing all uncertainty as a lack of faith, it is able to provide a clear link between all the Old Testament stories, and give them a fitting climax in the New Testament.

But it would be highly misleading to leave it at that. It is dishonest to pretend that this is the Bible's only line of thought about faith. It also has texts that are far more ambiguous. Interestingly enough, they are centred on the very personalities listed above.

Take Abraham. If he is the model of unquestioning faith, why is it that the text which praises his faith (Genesis 15:6) is sandwiched between two stories in which he asks some very worried questions about his lack of children (15:1-5) and his lack of landed property (15:8)? Is he as untroubled as he is depicted when he goes out into the unknown? Is he as sanguine about the sacrifice of Isaac as we imagine, or totally uncertain both before and after the event whether his God demands the same kind of child-sacrifice as the gods of his neighbours? In short, do the stories tell of the testing of a faith which remains perfectly serene before and after the test? Or do they tell of some deeper level, where his questions, doubts and anguish are part and parcel of a faith which necessarily involves ambiguity and tension?

Or take Moses. The classical portrait idealises him. He is a man of such strong faith that he alone, of all people, sees God and speaks with him face to face. What of the pathos of the parallel story which shows him pleading for a vision of God's face, and having to make do with a glimpse of his back as he crouches in his cranny (Exodus 33:18-23)? And what of the strange tradition suggesting that his final failure to enter the Promised Land was due to a 'breaking of faith' (Deuteronomy 32:51-52)? Did he break faith, or does faith necessarily involve this kind of ambiguity?

The prophets are happily quoted as shining examples of faith, the champions who remained certain when everyone else wavered. Yet they operated alongside people later labelled as false prophets, who preached with an even greater confidence and certainty. In fact, the mark of true prophets seems to be their honest admission of a lack of ultimate certainty. Elijah in his lonely desolation travels all the way to Mount Horeb, only to find that even there he has difficulty in discerning the voice of his God (1 Kings 19:1-12). Jeremiah's private diary reveals a heart torn between confidence and despair:

> Woe is me, my mother, that you bore me,
> a man of strife and contention to the whole land! …
> Lord … remember me and visit me,
> and take vengeance for me on my persecutors.
> In thy forbearance take me not away;
> know that for thy sake I bear reproach.
> Thy words were found, and I ate them,
> and thy words became to me a joy
> and the delight of my heart;

for I am called by thy name,
O Lord, God of hosts…
Why [then] is my pain unceasing,
my wound incurable, refusing to be healed?
(Jeremiah 15:10-18)

Behold, they say to me,
'Where is the word of the Lord? Let it come!'
I have not pressed thee to send evil,
nor have I desired the day of disaster,
thou knowest;
that which came out of my lips
was before thy face.
Be not a terror to me.
(Jeremiah 17:15-17)

O Lord, thou hast deceived me, and I was deceived;
thou art stronger than I, and thou hast prevailed.
I have become a laughing stock all the day;
everyone mocks me… and the word of the Lord has become
for me a reproach and derision all day long…

Cursed be the day on which I was born!…
Cursed be the man who brought the news to my father,
'A son is born to you'…
[Why did he] not kill me in the womb?
So my mother would have been my grave,
and her womb for ever great.
Why did I come forth from the womb
to see toil and sorrow,
and spend my days in shame?
(Jeremiah 20:7-8, 14-18)

Jeremiah was a man of faith, none greater. The shattering
questions he asks, and the agonising struggle with God – these
are not incompatible with faith, but its essential ingredients.

The same agony marks page after page of the psalms and the Wisdom literature, where the most awkward questions are asked about the traditional bland assumption that God rewards good and punishes evil. The psalmist's 'Whys?' and 'How longs?' are unashamedly presumed to be as valid a worship of God as his 'Hallelujahs!'. Job, the paragon of faith, conducts his dialogue with God in language which no theological journal would tolerate:

How can I answer him,
choosing my words with him?
Though I am innocent, I cannot answer him;
I must appeal for mercy to my accuser.
If I summoned him and he answered me,
I would not believe that he was listening to my voice.
For he crushes me with a tempest,
and multiplies my wounds without cause;
he will not let me get my breath,
but fills me with bitterness.
If it is a contest of strength, behold him!
If it is a matter of justice, who can summon him?...
Though I am blameless, he would prove me perverse...
he destroys both the blameless and the wicked.
When disaster brings sudden death,
he mocks at the calamity of the innocent.
(Job 9:14-23)

The faith of people like Job is more of a raging sea than a calm lake. They continue to believe when everything they once believed has been shattered, and when they have been stripped not only of all their possessions, but even of the explanation of why they ever had possessions in the first place.

## The faith of Jesus

When Jesus comes as the climax to this line of thought, he is no longer (as he was in the earlier exercise) simply an object of faith. He is himself a man of faith like all the others in the procession, a final illustration of what it means to be a believer in God. Being human, he sees no more clearly and no further than human beings can see. Like Abraham, Moses, Jeremiah and Job, he has to walk by faith, in the dark. True, there are stories which tell of the vigour and conviction with which he preached, and of his reproach for those who lacked his confidence in God. But there are also stories which tell of the battle he had to fight with Satan before he began his preaching career, of the agonising struggle with himself which made him sweat till he seemed to bleed with it, and of the cry of godforsaken despair with which he breathed his last. He is not to be deified by his followers, the epistle to the Hebrews insists, as if he did not share their human condition; he is with them on their painful march, as the 'pioneer of (their) faith' (Hebrews 12:2):

> We have not a high priest who is unable to sympathise with
> our weaknesses,
> but one who in every respect has been tempted as we are…
> He can deal gently with the ignorant and wayward,
> since he himself is beset with weakness…
> Jesus offered up prayers and supplications,
> with loud cries and tears…
> Although he was a Son,
> he learned obedience through what he suffered.
> (Hebrews 4:15-5:8)

As the New Testament tells it, the faith of Jesus' followers shared this ambiguity. In one sense, their faith was a joyful certainty, or at least developed into certainty, as they discovered that no one had ever spoken as Jesus had done, and that there was no one else to whom they would wish to turn to hear the words of life (John 6:68). Yet, in another sense, this faith of theirs was completely shattered when he died. They had thought he was the one who would bring about the

Kingdom of God – and now it was obvious that he wasn't (Luke 24:21). And that shattered faith had to be picked up and painfully rebuilt, as presumably all Christians discover over and over again, when they encounter the cross of Christ in their lives. While the pilgrimage of faith continues, we see only darkly, and know only in part (1 Corinthians 13:12).

## *Ambiguity*

So we find there remains considerable ambiguity. The meaning of the word 'faith' is much less clear-cut than we would like it to have been. We thought it meant certainty, but on analysis it seems to involve much uncertainty and searching. We thought it meant clarity, but on analysis it seems to involve much anguished groping in the dark. We thought it denoted something as steadfast and unmoving as a rock. On analysis it seems to demand that we move from positions we had hitherto never questioned, or faith will no longer be faith.

In short, faith can often look like the very opposite – a lack of faith. One might have been tempted to ask Jeremiah when circumstances crushed him, or Job when he put his devastating questions, or Jesus when he uttered his anguished cry, or the apostles when Calvary made them despair: 'Why don't you have more faith?' One would have been a fool to ask. To be crushed and questioning, to be anguished and despairing – these are part of what faith involves. And perhaps people should be made more aware that this is so, lest they feel a sense of guilt about their own questioning. There is an arrogance about the certainty of some believers which suggests that they are closing their eyes to whole areas of the Bible. According to the Bible, God is as much present in our doubts and questions as he is in our assurance. Perhaps more so: one can be too 'sure' of God to recognise where he is really at work.

Why should faith be so ambiguous, so ambivalent, so

unclear? The answer, in the last analysis, is very simple. Because faith is faith in God, and God by definition is the ultimate mystery.

When we try to define God, to pin him down, we are admitting that we find such mystery uncomfortable. Yet mystery is what God remains, and he defies all our efforts to make him manageable. To stand before such a God is a constant surprise and a constant challenge. To accept such a God is to find one's life radically altered, and continually subject to alteration. To believe in such a God is to accept that henceforth nothing is safe from him, that nothing can escape the transformation he works.

Faith is always a search, a struggle to understand. If there is no searching, what we've got is a lack of faith.

## Questions for Discussion

- 'Jesus is himself a man of faith…seeing no more clearly than human beings can see.' Does such a Jesus appeal to you or appal you?

- Since real faith makes enormous demands, religious people easily look for something more suitable as a substitute for faith. List some of these alternatives.

- Which is worse, credulity or lack of faith?

# Postscript

The aim of this book has been to highlight the *pluriformity* and *relativity* of the Bible.

A Bible that is *pluriform* (rather than uniform) does not speak with one voice on all the topics it deals with. It speaks with at least two voices, occasionally with several. In the chapters of this book we have considered some concrete examples of this. On subjects like violence, peace, poverty, providence, worldliness, faith, eschatology, forgiveness and so on, the Bible offers us advice that can only be called ambiguous. This is to say that, on subjects like these, no one is entitled to claim that 'the Bible teaches'. For every text that 'teaches' one view, a text can be found that 'teaches' the opposite. On a whole number of topics, the Bible speaks not with one voice but with several. It is not uniform but pluriform.

But as well as being pluriform, the Bible is also *relative*. Which is to say that its pronouncements can never be treated as absolute, final, definitive, eternal.

Why should this be so? Because it was written by limited human beings. However 'inspired' we may wish to claim these human beings to have been, they remain people of their own time, time-bound, inexorably marked by the knowledge and ignorance, by the world-view and prejudices of that time. God could not have made his eternal word truly 'incarnate' without accepting these human limitations. An absolute in human disguise would not be a genuine incarnation. It would be a cuckoo in the nest.

That is a second reason why no statement of the Bible can be quoted with the simple rubric 'The Bible says'. Even if the Bible were to speak with a single voice on a given topic, that single voice cannot be regarded as the last word. No human comment on any topic can ever be taken as the last word. How could the Bible's views on women's place in church ever have been taken as an absolute, when what it says about speaking in tongues was summarily dismissed as an outdated first century oddity? Surely both comments are relative to the circumstances in which they were written. Neither comment can be used to determine how Christians should live their faith in the twentieth and twenty-first centuries.

All this may seem to diminish the Bible, to demote it. 'It's not uniform but pluriform. So don't pay too much attention to what it says here; it may say something totally different elsewhere.' 'It's not absolute but relative. So don't pay too much attention to what it says anywhere; it's only the view of someone living in the tenth century BC, or first century AD.'

Demoting the Bible is not my aim. I continue to regard it as essential reading. I continue to regard it as a collection of the extraordinarily rich insights granted through the ages to the family to which I am proud to belong. Without insights like these I would be like a blind man. These insights are the guidelines without which I would not know where I stem from, or even where I am.

But I can never regard even these essential insights as absolute or final. They are the insights of other people, and they cannot really direct my life until they become my insights. How can I, as a Christian, turn Paul into the Great Lawgiver to whose every word I must bow, when his whole life was dedicated to attacking law as a way of life?

Even Jesus, for all the authority he easily assumed in his teaching, refused to lord it over his audience. Again and again he left it to his hearers to make up their own minds. Go through one of the Gospels and note the number of times Jesus is quoted as using a questioning technique in his teaching. I have found around sixty examples in the Gospel of Matthew alone ('What can make savourless salt salty again?' 'Are you not worth more than sparrows?' 'Why draw attention to the speck in your brother's eye?' 'Would you give your son a stone instead of bread?' for example.) Sometimes Jesus is represented as asking up to six questions in the same breath. I presume Mark and Luke could return a similar score.

This method of teaching continues even into Jesus' passion ('If this happens in the green wood, what will happen in the dry?') and the Easter Christ still talks in the same tones ('Was it not necessary that the Messiah should suffer?') It is interesting that John's much more magisterial Christ has few examples of this teaching technique.

Presumably the inference is that what was most typical of Jesus' teaching was its non-directive method. He challenged people to come to their own conclusions. Indeed the record is that he did much of his teaching in stories. All stories are open-ended. Hearers must make up their own minds about how they apply.

I imagine Jesus would have warmed to the story of the learned man who complained to the Buddha that the things he was teaching were not to be found in the holy Scriptures. 'Then put them in the Scriptures,' replied the Buddha.

'But some of the things you say actually contradict the Scriptures!'

'Then amend the Scriptures.'

Like the Sabbath, the Scriptures were made for man, not man for the Scriptures.

The Bible, what does it really say? In the light of the reflections that have occupied the preceding pages, it says that we must make up our own minds.

# Acknowledgements

The publishers wish to express their gratitude to the following for permission to include copyright material in this book:

Mrs Dale for the Bible translations by A. J. Dale, taken from *New World: The Heart of the New Testament*, OUP 1997.

Mr Peter De Rosa for the extracts from *Prayers for Pagans and Hypocrites*, London 1989.

*The Ecologist* for the extract from their November 1974 edition by A. Darlington.

HarperCollins Publishers, 77-85 Fulham Palace Road, London, W6 8JB for the extract from *Book of Witnesses* by David Kossoff (Fount, 1978).

The Institute of Contextual Theology, S. Africa, for the extract from *The Kairos Document*, 1985.

Mr Gary MacEoin for the extract from *Memoirs and Memories*, published by Twenty-Third Publications, USA, 1986.

Stainer & Bell Ltd, PO Box 110, Victoria House, 23 Gruneisen Road, Finchley, London, N3 1DZ for the poems *In the Present Tense* from 'The Two Way Clock' by Sydney Carter, S&B 1969 and *Over this dead loss to society*, about the work of Mother Teresa, S&B 1972.

The World Council of Churches, Geneva for the extract from their paper *Programme to Combat Racism*, December 1977.

Chapter 12 'On being perfect' was originally published in *The Newman Magazine*.